E. M Myers

The Centurial

A Jewish Calendar For One Hundred Years

E. M Myers

The Centurial
A Jewish Calendar For One Hundred Years

ISBN/EAN: 9783337030025

Printed in Europe, USA, Canada, Australia, Japan

Cover: Foto ©ninafisch / pixelio.de

More available books at **www.hansebooks.com**

THE CENTURIAL.

A JEWISH CALENDAR

FOR

ONE HUNDRED YEARS.

COMPILED BY

REV. E. M. MYERS,
167 EAST 74th STREET, NEW YORK CITY.

WITH A SUMMARY OF NEARLY SEVEN HUNDRED EVENTS OF HISTORY FROM THE
TIME OF THE CREATION TO THE PRESENT YEAR.

NEW YORK, 1891.
STETTINER, LAMBERT & Co., Printers.
THE BLOCH PRINTING AND PUBLISHING Co., Publishers,
CINCINNATI AND CHICAGO.

1890.

Tishri	1	First Day of New Year	Monday	Sept.	15
"	3	Fast of Gedaliah	Wednesday	"	17
"	10	Yom-Kippoor	Wednesday	"	24
"	15	First Day of Tabernacle	Monday	"	29
"	21	Hoshaunah-Rabbah	Sunday	Oct.	5
"	22	Sh'mini-Atseres	Monday	"	6
"	23	Simchas Torah	Tuesday	"	7
Cheshvan.		Rosh-Chodesh	Tues.-Wed.	"	14-15
Kislev	1	Rosh-Chodesh	Thursday	Nov.	13
"	25	First Day of Chanukah	Sunday	Dec.	7
Tebet	1	Rosh-Chodesh	Friday	"	12
"	10	Fast of Tebet	Sunday	"	21

1891.

Sh'vat	1	Rosh-Chodesh	Saturday	Jan.	10
Adar.		Rosh-Chodesh	Sun.-Mon.	Feb.	8 9
2d Adar.		Rosh Chodesh	Tues.-Wed.	Mar.	10-11
"	13	Fast of Esther	Monday.	"	23
"	14-15	Purim	Tues.-Wed.	"	24 25
Nissan	1	Rosh Chodesh	Thursday	April	9
"	15	First Day of Passover	Thursday	"	23
Iyar.		Rosh Chodesh	Fri.-Sat.	May	8-9
"	18	Lag-B'Omer	Tuesday	"	26
Sivan	1	Rosh-Chodesh	Sunday	June	7
"	6	First Day of Pentecost	Friday	"	12
Tammuz.		Rosh Chodesh	Mon.-Tues.	July	6-7
"	17	Fast of Tammuz	Thursday	"	23
Av	1	Rosh-Chodesh	Wednesday	Aug.	5
"	9	Fast of Av	Thursday	"	13
Ellul.		Rosh-Chodesh	Thurs.-Fri.	Sept.	3-4

EVENTFUL RECORDS.

A. M. 1656.—The Deluge.

" 18.—The birth of ABRAHAM.

" /0.—The confusion of language at the building of the tower of Babel, in the reign of SEMIRAMIS.

" 2018.—GOD's covenant with ABRAHAM.

" 2047.—Circumcision ordered.

" 2048.—The birth of ISAAC.

" 2074.—The offering of ISAAC at Mount Moriah.

" 2185.—JACOB obtained the blessing, for which he had to flee from the wrath of ESAU.

2

PENAL LAWS AGAINST THE JEWS.

WHILE the Jews have so much reason to be proud of their present position in England, ti may be interesting to refer to the restrictions under which they existed in times now happily past. We quote, in the first instance, the Penal Laws enunciated in Anno 7 Edward I., 1279.

1. No Jew shall come to or depart from England, without license, on pain of death.

2. No Jew shall walk or ride without a yellow badge upon his or her outward or upper garment, on pain of death.

3. No Jew shall contemn Jesus Christ, nor blaspheme His Divinity, on pain of being burnt.

4. No Jew shall stir out of his house or lodgings on Good Friday.

5. No Jew shall strike a Christian, on pain of having his right arm cut off.

6. No Jew shall kill a Christian, on pain that he be hanged alive on a gibbet, and be fed daily with bread and water, till he dies upon the same gibbet.

7. If any Jew shall cheat a Christian, and escape, all the rest of the Jews shall make satisfaction to the Christian so cheated.

8. All the Synagogues of the Jews shall be suppressed; and if any of their Rabbis or Priests shall teach or preach against the Christian religion hereafter, in England, all such preachers or teachers shall be burnt.

9. No Jew, on pain of hanging, shall transport any bullion or coin beyond the seas, nor deface nor melt down any Christian coin.

10. The King's Judges shall not hear the testimony of a Jew against a Christian.

11. No Jew shall be sworn upon the Evangelist.

12. The Jew shall have four judges, two whereof Christians, and the other Jews, who shall try and determine all causes between Jews and Christians.

13. All the children of Jews, as soon as born, the rector or vicar of the parish shall take from them, put such to nurses, and breed them up in the Christian religion, for which the Jews must pay all the charges.

14. In the Exchequer appointed for the Jews, there shall be half Christians and half Jews, and they shall both have equal power, and different locks and keys, to prevent fraud.

15. The Jews shall account for all the money they lay out, and for the profits, and return, before the justiciaries over the Jews, as often a y shall be required.

16. If any Jew shall be converted to the Christian Faith, all his usurious acquisition to be converted to pious and charitable uses; but all his goods, estate, or movables shall be his own, and not the King's as formerly accustomed.

17. The Jews shall go to hear Christian doctrine once a week, and as many English Jews as turn Christians shall be as free of England as if they were born of Christian parents.

18. No Jew shall cohabit with a Christian woman.

19. No Jew shall be buried in any consecrated ground.

		1891.			
Tishri	1	First Day of New Year...........	Saturday	Oct.	3
"	3	Fast of Gedaliah	Monday	"	5
"	10	Yom-Kippoor...................	Monday	"	12
"	15	First Day of Tabernacle.........	Saturday	"	17
"	21	Hoshannah-Rabbah.............	Friday	"	23
"	22	Sh'mini-Atseres................	Saturday	"	24
"	23	Simchas Torah.................	Sunday	"	25
Cheshvan.		Rosh-Chodesh	Sun.-Mon.	Nov.	1-2
Kislev	1	Rosh-Chodesh	Tues.-Wed.	Dec.	1 2
"	25	First Day of Chanukah	Saturday	"	26
		1892.			
Tebet	1	Rosh-Chodesh	Thurs.-Fri.	"	31
				Jan.	1
"	10	Fast of Tebet..................	Sunday	"	10
Sh'vat	1	Rosh-Chodesh	Saturday	"	30
Adar.		Rosh-Chodesh	Sun.-Mon.	Feb.	28-29
"	13	Fast of Esther.................	Saturday*	March	12
"	14-15	Purim	Sun.-Mon.	"	13-14
Nissan	1	Rosh-Chodesh	Tuesday	"	29
"	15	First Day of Passover	Tuesday	April	12
Iyar.		Rosh-Chodesh	Wed.-Thurs.	"	27-28
"	18	Lag-B'Omer...................	Sunday	May	15
Sivan	1	Rosh-Chodesh	Friday	"	27
"	6	First Day of Pentecost..........	Wednesday	June	1
Tammuz.		Rosh-Chodesh	Sat.-Sun.	"	25-26
"	17	Fast of Tammuz...............	Tuesday	July	12
Av	1	Rosh-Chodesh	Monday	"	25
"	9	Fast of Av	Tuesday	Aug.	2
Ellul.		Rosh-Chodesh	Tues.-Wed.	"	23-24

* Observed Thursday previous.

EVENTFUL RECORDS.

A. M. 2216.—JOSEPH sold by his brethren.

" 2229 —JOSEPH interpreted PHARAOH's dream.

" 2368.—The birth of MOSES.

" 2448.—The Decalogue was given on MOUNT SINAI.

MOSES ascended the Mount and received the Oral Law.

The Molten Calf made and worshipped.

A census of the male population over 20 years of age was taken by a tax of half a shekel, to defray the expenses of the Tabernacle, which was completed on the first of *Tishri,* 2450.

4

		1892.			
Tishri	1	First Day of New Year.........	Thursday	Sept.	22
"	3	Fast of Gedaliah................	Saturday*	"	24
"	10	Yom-Kippoor	Saturday	Oct.	1
"	15	First Day of Tabernacle	Thursday	"	6
"	21	Hoshaunah-Rabbah	Wednesday	"	12
"	22	Sh'mini Atseres...............	Thursday	"	13
"	23	Simchas Torah.................	Friday	"	14
Cheshvan.		Rosh-Chodesh	Fri.-Sat.	"	21-22
Kislev	1	Rosh-Chodesh	Sunday	Nov.	20
"	25	First Day of Chanukah	Wednesday	Dec.	14
Tebet		Rosh-Chodesh	Mon.-Tues.	"	19-20
"	10	Fast of Tebet.................	Thursday	"	29
		1893.			
Sh'vat	1	Rosh-Chodesh	Wednesday	Jan.	18
Adar.		Rosh-Chodesh	Thurs.-Fri.	Feb.	16-17
"	13	Fast of Esther................	Wednesday	Mar.	1
"	14-15	Purim	Thurs.-Fri.	"	2-3
Nissan	1	Rosh Chodesh	Saturday	"	18
"	15	First Day of Passover...........	Saturday	April	1
Iyar.		Rosh Chodesh	Sun.-Mon.	"	16-17
"	18	Lag-B'Omer..................	Thursday	May	4
Sivan	1	Rosh-Chodesh..............	Tuesday	"	16
"	6	First Day of Pentecost.	Sunday	"	21
Tammuz.		Rosh-Chodesh	Wed.-Thurs.	June	14-15
"	17	Fast of Tammuz............. .	Saturday*	July	1
Av	1	Rosh-Chodesh	Friday	"	14
"	9	Fast of Av....	Saturday*	"	25
Ellul.		Rosh-Chodesh	Sat.-Sun.	Aug.	12-13

* Observed the day following.

EVENTFUL RECORDS.

A. M. 2487.—A rebellion arose amongst the people through want of water. Moses disobeyed the divine command by striking the rock instead of speaking to it, in consequence of which he was not permitted to enter the Holy Land.

Sihon, King of the Ammonites, and Og, King of Bashan, were vanquished and their territories divided between the tribes of Reuben, Gad, and half of Manasseh.

5654 A.M. 1893-'94 C.Æ.

		1893.	
Tishri	1	First Day of New Year...........	Monday
"	3	Fast of Gedaliah	Wednesday
"	10	Yom-Kippoor...................	Wednesday
"	15	First Day of Tabernacle.........	Monday
"	21	Hoshannah-Rabbah.............	Sunday
"	22	Sh'mini-Atseres................	Monday
"	23	Simchas Torah.................	Tuesday
Cheshvan.		Rosh-Chodesh	Tues.-Wed.
Kislev	1	Rosh-Chodesh	Thurs.-Fri.
"	25	First Day of Chanukah	Monday
Tebet	1	Rosh-Chodesh	Sat.-Sun.
"	10	Fast of Tebet..................	Tuesday
		1894.	
Sh'vat	1	Rosh-Chodesh	Monday
Adar.		Rosh-Chodesh	Tues.-Wed.
2d Adar.		Rosh-Chodesh	Thurs.-Fri.
"	13	Fast of Esther.................	Wednesday
"	14-15	Purim	Thurs.-Fri.
Nissan	1	Rosh-Chodesh	Saturday
"	15	First Day of Passover	Saturday
Iyar.		Rosh-Chodesh	Sun.-Mon.
"	18	Lag-B'Omer...................	Thursday
Sivan	1	Rosh-Chodesh	Tuesday
'	6	First Day of Pentecost..........	Sunday
Tammuz.		Rosh-Chodesh	Wed.-Thurs.
"	17	Fast of Tammuz................	Saturday*
Av	1	Rosh-Chodesh	Friday
"	9	Fast of Av	Saturday*
Ellul.		Rosh-Chodesh	Sat.-Sun.

* Observed the day following

EVENTFUL RECORDS.

A. M. 2448.—Moses died at the age of 120 years and was
Joshua, who was acknowledged as Judge of Is
his guidance, the Israelites crossed the Jordan,
Holy Land and made an alliance with the
Being attacked by five kings of surrounding pec
organized an army and went to their assistan
battle, it is recorded in Scripture, he prayed t
might remain stationary until he had complete

" 2503.—An equitable division of Palestine was made
amongst the remaining nine and a half tribes.

8

KRAKAUER

PIANOS

		1894.			
Tishri	1	First Day of New Year..........	Monday	Oct.	1
"	3	Fast of Gedaliah	Wednesday	"	3
"	10	Yom-Kippoor	Wednesday	"	10
"	15	First Day of Tabernacle	Monday	"	15
"	21	Hoshannah-Rabbah	Sunday	"	21
"	22	Sh'mini Atseres.................	Monday	"	22
"	23	Simchas Torah..................	Tuesday	"	23
Cheshvan.		Rosh-Chodesh	Tues.-Wed.	"	30-31
Kislev	1	Rosh-Chodesh	Thursday	Nov.	29
"	25	First Day of Chanukah	Sunday	Dec.	23
Tebet	1	Rosh-Chodesh	Friday	"	28
		1895.			
"	10	Fast of Tebet...................	Sunday	Jan.	6
Sh'vat	1	Rosh-Chodesh	Saturday	"	26
Adar.		Rosh-Chodesh	Sun.-Mon.	Feb. 24 25	
"	13	Fast of Esther.................	Saturday*	Mar.	9
"	14-15	Purim	Sun.-Mon.	"	10-11
Nissan	1	Rosh Chodesh	Tuesday	"	26
"	15	First Day of Passover...........	Tuesday	April	9
Iyar.		Rosh-Chodesh	Wed.-Thurs.	"	24-25
"	18	Lag-B'Omer.....................	Sunday	May	12
Sivan	1	Rosh-Chodesh..................	Friday	"	24
"	6	First Day of Pentecost.	Wednesday	"	29
Tammuz.		Rosh-Chodesh	Sat.-Sun.	June 22-23	
"	17	Fast of Tammuz	Tuesday	July	9
Av	1	Rosh-Chodesh	Monday	"	22
"	9	Fast of Av	Tuesday	"	30
Ellul.		Rosh-Chodesh	Tues.-Wed.	Aug. 20-21	

* Observed Thursday previous.

EVENTFUL RECORDS.

A. M. 2516.—Having ruled Israel for twenty-eight years, JOSHUA died, aged 110 years, and was succeeded by OTHNIEL, who governed the nation forty years, the elders, however, assuming government during his administration.

"   2525.—In this year, anarchy and revolt took place. The tribes made war against the Benjamites, and Israel became tributary to CUSHAN-RISHATAYIM, King of MESOPOTAMIA.

"   2533.—They were released from paying further tribute by OTHNIEL, who fought against CUSHAN-RISHATAYIM, and defeated him.

WILHELM & GRAEF,

BROADWAY & 26th ST.,

NEW YORK,

IMPORTERS OF

CHINA, GLASS, & POTTERY

Dinner Services.................... from $15 00
Glass   "   60 Pieces......... "   5 50
Toilet Sets....................... "   2 50

Royal Dresden Figures and Groups.

*Royal Worcester, Derby, Minton,
Cauldon, etc., Ware.*

		1895.			
Tishri	1	First Day of New Year...........	Thursday	Sept.	19
"	3	Fast of Gedaliah	Saturday*	"	21
"	10	Yom-Kippoor...................	Saturday	"	28
"	15	First Day of Tabernacle.........	Thursday	Oct.	3
"	21	Hoshannah-Rabbah..............	Wednesday	"	9
"	22	Sh'mini-Atseres................	Thursday	"	10
"	23	Simchas Torah.................	Friday	"	11
Cheshvan.		Rosh-Chodesh	Fri.-Sat.	"	18-19
Kislev		Rosh-Chodesh	Sun.-Mon.	Nov.	17-18
"	25	First Day of Chanukah	Thursday	Dec.	12
Tebet		Rosh-Chodesh	Tues.-Wed.	"	17-18
"	10	Fast of Tebet...................	Friday	"	27
		1896.			
Sh'vat	1	Rosh-Chodesh	Thursday	Jan.	16
Adar.		Rosh-Chodesh	Fri.-Sat.	Feb.	14-15
"	13	Fast of Esther.................	Thursday	"	27
"	14-15	Purim	Fri.-Sat.	"	28-29
Nissan	1	Rosh-Chodesh	Sunday	March	15
"	15	First Day of Passover	Sunday	"	29
Iyar.		Rosh-Chodesh	Mon.-Tues.	Apr.	13-14
"	18	Lag-B'Omer...................	Friday	May	1
Sivan	1	Rosh-Chodesh	Wednesday	"	13
"	6	First Day of Pentecost..........	Monday	"	18
Tammuz.		Rosh-Chodesh	Thurs.-Fri.	June	11-12
"	17	Fast of Tammuz...............	Sunday	"	28
Av	1	Rosh-Chodesh	Saturday	July	11
"	9	Fast of Av	Sunday	"	19
Ellul.		Rosh-Chodesh	Sun.-Mon.	Aug.	9-10

* Observed the following day.

EVENTFUL RECORDS.

A. M. 2556.—OTHNIEL was succeeded by EHUD, who judged Israel eighty years.

" 2623.—EGLON, King of MOAB, having oppressed Israel for eighteen years, was assassinated by EHUD.

" 2635.—SHAMGAR, who was the fourth Judge in Israel, only ruled one year, during which he made war against the Philistines and defeated them.

		1896.			
Tishri	1	First Day of New Year	Tuesday	Sept.	8
"	3	Fast of Gedaliah	Thursday	"	10
"	10	Yom-Kippoor	Thursday	"	17
"	15	First Day of Tabernacle	Tuesday	"	22
"	21	Hoshaunah-Rabbah	Monday	"	28
"	22	Sh'mini Atseres	Tuesday	"	29
"	23	Simchas-Torah	Wednesday	"	30
Cheshvan.		Rosh-Chodesh	Wed.-Thurs.	Oct.	7-8
Kislev	1	Rosh-Chodesh	Friday	Nov.	6
"	25	First Day of Chanukah	Monday	"	30
Tebet		Rosh-Chodesh	Sat.-Sun.	Dec.	5-6
"	10	Fast of Tebet	Tuesday	"	15
		1897.			
Sh'vat	1	Rosh-Chodesh	Monday	Jan.	4
Adar.		Rosh-Chodesh	Tues.-Wed.	Feb.	2 3
2d Adar.		Rosh-Chodesh	Thurs.-Fri.	Mar.	4-5
"	13	Fast of Esther	Wednesday	"	17
"	14-15	Purim	Thurs.-Fri.	"	18-19
Nissan	1	Rosh Chodesh	Saturday	April	3
"	15	First Day of Passover	Saturday	"	17
Iyar.		Rosh-Chodesh	Sun.-Mon.	May	2-3
"	18	Lag-B'Omer	Thursday	"	20
Sivan	1	Rosh-Chodesh	Tuesday	June	1
"	6	First Day of Pentecost	Sunday	"	6
Tammuz.		Rosh-Chodesh	Wed.-Thurs.	{ " July	30 1
"	17	Fast of Tammuz	Saturday*	"	17
Av	1	Rosh-Chodesh	Friday	"	30
"	9	Fast of Av	Saturday*	Aug.	8
Ellul.		Rosh-Chodesh	Sat.-Sun.	"	28-29

* Observed the following day.

EVENTFUL RECORDS.

A. M. 2636.—DEBORAH became Judge and ruled for forty years. Aided by BARAK, she delivered the people from the tyranny and oppression of JABIN, King of Canaan. Her song of praise and triumph will be found in the fifth chapter of the book of Judges.

" 2676.—GIDEON appointed Judge and ruled for forty years. The MIDIANITES were defeated by him, after they had spoiled and laid the country waste for a period of seven years.

		1897.			
Tishri	1	First Day of New Year..........	Monday	Sept.	27
"	3	Fast of Gedaliah	Wednesday	"	29
"	10	Yom-Kippoor...................	Wednesday	Oct.	6
"	15	First Day of Tabernacle.........	Monday	"	11
"	21	Hoshannah-Rabbah..............	Sunday	"	17
"	22	Sh'mini-Atseres................	Monday	"	18
"	23	Simchas-Torah.................	Tuesday	"	19
Cheshvan.		Rosh-Chodesh	Tues.-Wed.	"	26-27
Kislev		Rosh-Chodesh	Thurs.-Fri.	Nov.	25-26
"	25	First Day of Chanukah	Monday	Dec.	20
Tebet		Rosh-Chodesh	Sat.-Sun.	"	25-26
		1898.			
"	10	Fast of Tebet..................	Tuesday	Jan.	4
Sh'vat	1	Rosh-Chodesh	Monday	"	24
Adar.		Rosh-Chodesh	Tues.-Wed.	Feb.	22-23
"	13	Fast of Esther.................	Monday	March	7
"	14-15	Purim	Tues.-Wed.	"	8-9
Nissan	1	Rosh-Chodesh	Thursday	"	24
"	15	First Day of Passover	Thursday	Apr.	7
Iyar.		Rosh-Chodesh	Fri.-Sat.	"	22-23
"	18	Lag-B'Omer...................	Tuesday	May	10
Sivan	1	Rosh-Chodesh	Sunday	"	22
"	6	First Day of Pentecost..........	Friday	"	27
Tammuz.		Rosh-Chodesh	Mon.-Tues.	June	20-21
"	17	Fast of Tammuz................	Thursday	July	7
Av	1	Rosh-Chodesh	Wednesday	"	20
"	9	Fast of Av	Thursday	"	28
Ellul.		Rosh-Chodesh	Thurs.-Fri.	Aug.	18-19

EVENTFUL RECORDS.

A. M. 2716.—ABIMELECH, GIDEON's son, assumed regal power and slew seventy of his brethren. JOTHAM, the youngest, hid himself and was thereby saved. After reigning three years, ABIMELECH led an attack against THEBEZ, during which he was killed by a heavy stone which was thrown on his head.

" 2719.—TOLANG, the eighth Judge, ruled twenty-three years and was succeeded by JAIR.

" 2742.—JAIR governed the nation for twenty-two years.

			1898.		
Tishri	1	First Day of New Year	Saturday	Sept.	17
"	3	Fast of Gedaliah...............	Monday	"	19
"	10	Yom-Kippoor..................	Monday	"	26
"	15	First Day of Tabernacle.........	Saturday	Oct.	1
"	21	Hoshannah-Rabbah.............	Friday	"	7
"	22	Sh'mini-Atseres................	Saturday	"	8
"	23	Simchas-Torah.................	Sunday	"	9
Cheshvan.		Rosh-Chodesh	Sun.-Mon.	"	16-17
Kislev	1	Rosh-Chodesh	Tuesday	Nov.	15
"	25	First Day of Chanukah	Friday	Dec.	9
Tebet	1	Rosh-Chodesh	Wednesday	"	14
"	10	Fast of Tebet..................	Friday	"	23
			1899.		
Sh'vat	1	Rosh-Chodesh	Thursday	Jan.	12
Adar.		Rosh-Chodesh	Fri.-Sat.	Feb.	10-11
"	13	Fast of Esther.................	Thursday	"	23
"	14-15	Purim........................	Fri.-Sat.	"	24-25
Nissan	1	Rosh-Chodesh	Sunday	Mar.	12
"	15	First Day of Passover	Sunday	"	26
Iyar.		Rosh-Chodesh	Mon.-Tues.	Apr.	10-11
"	18	Lag-B'Qmer........	Friday	"	28
Sivan	1	Rosh-Chodesh	Wednesday	May	10
"	6	First Day of Pentecost...........	Monday	"	15
Tammuz.		Rosh-Chodesh	Thurs.-Fri.	June	8-9
"	17	Fast of Tammuz................	Sunday	"	25
Av	1	Rosh-Chodesh	Saturday	July	8
"	9	Fast of Av....................	Sunday	"	16
Ellul.		Rosh-Chodesh	Sun.-Mon.	Aug.	6-7

EVENTFUL RECORDS.

A. M. 2764.—The AMMONITES began to oppress Israel.

" 2781.—The people appealed to JEPHTAH to lead an army against the Ammonites, and promised to make him ruler, if successful. He obtained a complete victory and governed Israel for six years. His vow, previous to going out to battle, is recorded in the book of Judges, xi. 31. A more correct translation of it, however, and one entirely in accordance with the Hebrew text, would substitute the word *or*, instead of *and*, which would made it read, "*or* I will offer it," etc. This was probably what he intended to signify; that if fit, it should be sacrificed, *or* should be consecrated to God's service.

18

		1899.			
Tishri	1	First Day of New Year	Tuesday	Sept.	5
"	3	Fast of Gedaliah................	Thursday	"	7
"	10	Yom-Kippoor...................	Thursday	"	14
"	15	First Day of Tabernacle.........	Tuesday	"	19
"	21	Hoshannah-Rabbah..............	Monday	".	25
"	22	Sh'mini-Atseres................	Tuesday	"	26
"	23	Simchas-Torah..................	Wednesday	"	27
Cheshvan.		Rosh-Chodesh	Wed.-Thurs.	Oct.	4-5
Kislev	1	Rosh-Chodesh	Friday	Nov.	3
"	25	First Day of Chanukah..........	Monday	"	27
Tebet.		Rosh-Chodesh	Sat.-Sun.	Dec.	2-3
"	10	Fast of Tebet..................	Tuesday	"	12
		1900.			
Sh'vat	1	Rosh-Chodesh	Monday	Jan.	1
Adar.		Rosh-Chodesh	Tues.-Wed.	"	30-31
2d Adar.		Rosh-Chodesh	Thurs.-Fri.	Mar.	1-2
"	13	Fast of Esther.................	Wednesday	"	14
"	14-15	Purim.........................	Thurs.-Fri.	"	15-16
Nissan	1	Rosh-Chodesh	Saturday	"	31
"	15	First Day of Passover..........	Saturday	April	14
Iyar.		Rosh-Chodesh	Sun.-Mon.	"	29-30
"	18	Lag-B'Omer....................	Thursday	May	17
Sivan	1	Rosh-Chodesh	Tuesday	"	29
"	6	First Day of Pentecost..........	Sunday	June	3
Tammuz.		Rosh-Chodesh	Wed.-Thurs.	"	27-28
"	17	Fast of Tammuz	Saturday*	July	15
Av	1	Rosh-Chodesh	Friday	"	27
"	9	Fast of Av....................	Saturday*	Aug.	4
Ellul.		Rosh-Chodesh	Sat.-Sun.	"	25-26

* Observed the following day.

EVENTFUL RECORDS.

A. M. 2787.—IBZAN, otherwise named BOAZ, who espoused RUTH, governed Israel for seven years.

" 2793.—ELON, the twelfth Judge, ruled ten years.

" 2803.—ABDON succeeded ELON and governed eight years.

" 2811.—SAMSON, celebrated for his extraordinary strength, was Judge for twenty years. Through the treachery of his wife, DELILAH, he was overcome by the Philistines, who put out his eyes and made sport of him. Whilst thus engaged at one of their feasts, in their temple, SAMSON, who had been placed between the two main pillars of the building, prayed to God to give him back his strength. His prayer being answered, he snapped the pillars in twain, the roof fell in, killing him with his tormentors.

		1900.			
Tishri	1	First Day of New Year..........	Monday	Sept.	24
"	3	Fast of Gedaliah	Wednesday	"	26
"	10	Yom-Kippoor...................	Wednesday	Oct.	3
"	15	First Day of Tabernacle.........	Monday	"	8
"	21	Hoshannah-Rabbah.............	Sunday	"	14
"	22	Sh'mini-Atscres................	Monday	"	15
"	23	Simchas-Torah.................	Tuesday	".	16
Cheshvan.		Rosh-Chodesh	Tues.-Wed.	"	23-24
Kislev		Rosh-Chodesh	Thurs.-Fri.	Nov.	22-23
"	25	First Day of Chanukah	Monday	Dec.	17
Tebet		Rosh-Chodesh	Sat.-Sun.	"	22-23
		1901.			
"	10	Fast of Tebet..................	Tuesday	Jan.	1
Sh'vat	1	Rosh-Chodesh	Monday	"	21
Adar.		Rosh-Chodesh	Tues.-Wed.	Feb.	19-20
"	13	Fast of Esther.................	Monday	March	4
"	14-15	Purim	Tues.-Wed.	"	5-6
Nissan	1	Rosh-Chodesh	Thursday	"	21
"	15	First Day of Passover	Thursday	Apr.	4
Iyar.		Rosh-Chodesh	Fri.-Sat.	"	19-20
"	18	Lag-B'Omer...................	Tuesday	May	7
Sivan	1	Rosh-Chodesh	Sunday	"	19
"	6	First Day of Pentecost..........	Friday	"	24
Tammuz.		Rosh-Chodesh	Mon.-Tues.	June	17-18
"	17	Fast of Tammuz................	Thursday	July	4
Av	1	Rosh-Chodesh	Wednesday	"	17
"	9	Fast of Av	Thursday	"	25
Ellul.		Rosh-Chodesh	Thurs.-Fri.	Aug.	15-16

EVENTFUL RECORDS.

A.M.   2831.—The government now devolved upon ELI, the High Priest, who judged the nation for forty years, although during his government SAUL was anointed, by the prophet SAMUEL, to be his successor.

"   2854.—The birth of DAVID.

"   2864.—SAUL anointed by SAMUEL to be king, after ELI's death.

"   2871.—The Ark of the Covenant taken in battle by the Philistines. On hearing this, and that his two sons had been killed, ELI, who was very old, fell from his chair and died. SAMUEL, the prophet, acted as Judge until his death, which occurred in 2882, SAUL being king.

THE

Mercantile National Bank

OF THE CITY OF NEW YORK.

191 BROADWAY.

CAPITAL, - - - - $1,000,000

SURPLUS AND PROFITS, - 950,000

WM. P. ST. JOHN, - PRESIDENT.

FRED'K B. SCHENCK, CASHIER.

JAMES V. LOTT, - ASS'T CASHIER.

DIRECTORS:

CHARLES T. BARNEY,   GEORGE H. SARGENT,

WILLIAM C. BROWNING,   CHARLES M. VAIL,

CHARLES L. COLBY,   ISAAC WALLACH,

GEORGE W. CROSSMAN,   JAMES W. WENTZ,

HENRY T. KNEELAND,   FRANCIS H. N. WHITING,

EMANUEL LEHMAN,   RICHARD H. WILLIAMS,

SETH M. MILLIKEN,   FREDERICK B. SCHENCK,

WILLIAM P. ST. JOHN.

This Bank solicits accounts from Individuals, Firms, and Corporations.

			1901.			
Tishri	1	First Day of New Year	Saturday	Sept.	14
"	3	Fast of Gedaliah	Monday	"	16
"	10	Yom-Kippoor	Monday	"	23
"	15	First Day of Tabernacle	Saturday	"	28
"	21	Hoshannah-Rabbah	Friday	Oct.	4
"	22	Sh'mini Atseres	Saturday	"	5
"	23	Simchas-Torah	Sunday	"	6
Cheshvan.		Rosh-Chodesh	Sun.-Mon.	"	13-14
Kislev	1	Rosh-Chodesh	Tuesday	Nov.	12
"	25	First Day of Chanukah	Friday	Dec.	6
Tebet	1	Rosh-Chodesh	Monday	"	11
"	10	Fast of Tebet	Friday	"	20

			1902.			
Sh'vat	1	Rosh-Chodesh	Thursday	Jan.	9
Adar.		Rosh-Chodesh	Fri.-Sat.	Feb.	7 8
2d Adar.		Rosh-Chodesh	Sun.-Mon.	Mar.	9-10
"	13	Fast of Esther	Saturday*	"	22
"	14-15	Purim	Sun.-Mon.	"	23-24
Nissan	1	Rosh Chodesh	Tuesday	April	8
"	15	First Day of Passover	Tuesday	"	22
Iyar.		Rosh-Chodesh	Wed.-Thurs.	May	7-8
"	18	Lag-B'Omer	Sunday	"	25
Sivan	1	Rosh-Chodesh	Friday	June	6
"	6	First Day of Pentecost	Wednesday	"	11
Tammuz.		Rosh-Chodesh	Sat.-Sun.	July	5-6
"	17	Fast of Tammuz	Tuesday	"	22
Av	1	Rosh-Chodesh	Monday	Aug.	4
"	9	Fast of Av	Tuesday	"	12
Ellul.		Rosh-Chodesh	Tues.-Wed.	Sept.	2-3

* Observed Thursday previous.

EVENTFUL RECORDS.

A.M. 2876.—SAMUEL anointed DAVID to succeed to the kingdom.

" 2877.—DAVID slew GOLIATH, which increased the already existing jealousy of SAUL against him.

" 2884.—The Philistines defeated SAUL in battle and wounded him. SAUL could not bear the humiliation and killed himself. DAVID was then declared king of Judah. ISH-BOSHETH, one of SAUL's sons, raised a civil war, but was murdered in his bed. When the assassins brought his head to DAVID, he denounced the cold-blooded murder of a defenceless man, even of an enemy, and had them slain.

SAUL AND DAVID.

		1902.			
Tishri	1	First Day of New Year	Thursday	Oct.	2
"	3	Fast of Gedaliah................	Saturday*	"	4
"	10	Yom-Kippoor...................	Saturday	"	11
"	15	First Day of Tabernacle.........	Thursday	"	16
"	21	Iloshannah-Rabbah..............	Wednesday	"	22
"	22	Sh'mini-Atseres................	Thursday	"	23
"	23	Simchas-Torah..................	Friday	"	24
Cheshvan.		Rosh-Chodesh *.......	{ Friday	"	31
			{ Saturday	Nov.	1
Kislev		Rosh-Chodesh	{ Sunday	"	30
			{ Monday	Dec.	1
"	25	First Day of Chanukah.........	Thursday	"	25
Tebet.		Rosh-Chodesh.................	Tues.-Wed.	"	30-31
		1903.			
"	10	Fast of Tebet..................	Friday	Jan.	9
Sh'vat	1	Rosh-Chodesh	Thursday	"	29
Adar.		Rosh-Chodesh	Fri.-Sat.	Feb. 27-28	
"	13	Fast of Esther.................	Thursday	Mar.	12
"	14	Purim........................	Fri.-Sat.	"	13-14
Nissan	1	Rosh-Chodesh	Sunday	"	29
"	15	First Day of Passover..........	Sunday	April	12
Iyar.		Rosh-Chodesh	Mon.-Tues.	"	27-28
"	18	Lag-B'Omer.................... 33d day of Omer.	Friday	May	15
Sivan	1	Rosh-Chodesh	Wednesday	"	27
"	6	First Day of Pentecost.........	Monday	June	1
Tammuz.		Rosh-Chodesh	Thurs.-Fri.	"	25-26
"	17	Fast of Tammuz	Sunday	July	12
Av	1	Rosh-Chodesh	Saturday	"	25
"	9	Fast of Av....................	Sunday	Aug.	2
Ellul.		Rosh-Chodesh .....'..........	Sun.-Mon.	"	23-24

* Observed the following day.

EVENTFUL RECORDS.

A. M. 2892.—DAVID acknowledged king over all Israel.

" 2893.—Jerusalem taken possession of and constituted the seat of government.

" 2921.—DAVID being old, and his son ABSALOM wishing to succeed to the kingdom, rebelled.

" 2923.—ADONIJAH, also an aspirant for the throne, assumed regal authority, but DAVID publicly announced his son SOLOMON to be his successor.

" 2924.—DAVID died and SOLOMON ascended the throne.

5664 A.M. 1903-'4 C.Æ.

		1903.			
Tishri	1	First Day of New Year	Tuesday	Sept.	22
"	3	Fast of Gedaliah................	Thursday	"	24
"	10	Yom-Kippoor...................	Thursday	Oct.	1
"	15	First Day of Tabernacle.........	Tuesday	".	6
"	21	Hoshannah-Rabbah..............	Monday	"	12
"	22	Sh'mini-Atseres................	Tuesday	"	13
"	23	Simchas-Torah.................	Wednesday	"	14
Cheshvan.		Rosh-Chodesh	Wed.-Thurs.	"	21-22
Kislev	1	Rosh-Chodesh	Friday	Nov.	20
"	25	First Day of Chanukah	Monday	Dec.	14
Tebet.		Rosh-Chodesh	Sat.-Sun.	"	19-20
"	10	Fast of Tebet.................	Tuesday	"	29
		1904.			
Sh'vat	1	Rosh-Chodesh	Monday	Jan.	18
Adar.		Rosh-Chodesh	Tues.-Wed.	Feb.	16-17
"	13	Fast of Esther................	Monday	"	29
"	14	Purim.........................	Tues.-Wed.	Mar.	1-2
Nissan	1	Rosh-Chodesh	Thursday	"	17
"	15	First Day of Passover	Thursday	"	31
Iyar.		Rosh-Chodesh	Fri.-Sat.	Apr.	15-16
"	18	Lag-B'Omer .... 33d day of Omer.	Tuesday	May	3
Sivan	1	Rosh-Chodesh	Sunday	"	15
"	6	First Day of Pentecost..........	Friday	"	20
Tammuz		Rosh-Chodesh	Mon.-Tues.	June	13-14
"	17	Fast of Tammuz................	Thursday	"	30
Av	1	Rosh-Chodesh	Wednesday	July	13
"	9	Fast of Av....................	Thursday	"	21
Ellul.		Rosh-Chodesh	Sat.-Sun.	Aug.	11-12

EVENTFUL RECORDS.

A. M. 2925.—SOLOMON's celebrated judgment between the two claimants of the living child.

" 2928.—The building of the first Temple was commenced, four hundred and eighty years after the Exodus.

" 2935.—The Temple completed and dedicated on the twenty-third day of *Tishri.*

" 2961.—A revolt and rebellion took place, instigated and headed by JEROBOHAM, son of NEBAT.

1904.

Tishri	1	First Day of New Year..........	Saturday	Sept.	10
"	3	Fast of Gedaliah	Monday	"	12
"	10	Yom-Kippoor..................	Monday	"	19
"	15	First Day of Tabernacle.........	Saturday	"	24
"	21	Hoshannah-Rabbah.............	Friday	"	30
"	22	Sh'mini-Atseres................	Saturday	Oct.	1
"	23	Simchas-Torah.................	Sunday	"	2
Cheshvan.		Rosh-Chodesh	Sun.-Mon.	"	9-10
Kislev.		Rosh-Chodesh	Tues.-Wed.	Nov.	8-9
"	25	First Day of Chanukah	Saturday	Dec.	3
Tebet.		Rosh-Chodesh	Thurs.-Fri.	"	8-9
"	10	Fast of Tebet..................	Sunday	"	18

1905.

Sh'vat	1	Rosh-Chodesh	Saturday	Jan.	7
Adar.		Rosh-Chodesh	Sun.-Mon.	Feb.	5-6
2d Adar.		Rosh-Chodesh	Tues.-Wed.	Mar.	7-8
"	13	Fast of Esther.................	Monday	"	20
"	14-15	Purim	Tues.-Wed.	"	21-22
Nissan.		Rosh-Chodesh	Thursday	April	6
"	15	First Day of Passover	Thursday	"	20
Iyar.		Rosh-Chodesh	Fri.-Sat.	May	5-6
"	18	Lag-B'Omer...................	Tuesday	"	23
		33d day of Omer.			
Sivan.		Rosh-Chodesh	Sunday	June	4
"	6	First Day of Pentecost..........	Friday	"	9
Tammuz.		Rosh-Chodesh	Mon.-Tues.	July	3-4
"	17	Fast of Tammuz................	Thursday	"	20
Av	1	Rosh-Chodesh	Wednesday	Aug.	2
"	9	Fast of Av	Thursday	"	10
Ellul.		Rosh-Chodesh	Thurs.-Fri.	" / Sept.	31 / 1

EVENTFUL RECORDS.

A. M. 2964.—SOLOMON died, having reigned forty years. He was succeeded by his son REHOBOAM, who was so tyrannical that the nation became divided into two kingdoms and separate dynasties, namely, Israel and Judah. REHOBOAM continued King of Judah for seventeen years, JEROBOAM 1ST reigning over Israel twenty-two years.

" 2969.—Jerusalem was taken and the Temple plundered by SHISHKAH, King of Egypt.

" 2981.—REHOBOAM was succeeded by his son ABIJAH, who reigned three years.

1905.

Tishri	1	First Day of New Year	Saturday	Sept.	30
"	3	Fast of Gedaliah	Monday	Oct.	2
"	10	Yom-Kippoor	Monday	"	9
"	15	First Day of Tabernacle	Saturday	"	14
"	21	Hoshaunah-Rabbah	Friday	"	20
"	22	Sh'mini-Atseres	Saturday	"	21
"	23	Simchas-Torah	Sunday	"	22
Cheshvan.		Rosh-Chodesh	Sun.-Mon.	"	29-30
Kislev.		Rosh-Chodesh	Tues.-Wed.	Nov.	28-29
"	25	First Day of Chanukah	Saturday	Dec.	23
Tebet.		Rosh-Chodesh	Thurs.-Fri.	"	28-29

1906.

"	10	Fast of Tebet	Sunday	Jan.	7
Sh'vat	1	Rosh-Chodesh	Saturday	"	27
Adar.		Rosh-Chodesh	Sun.-Mon.	Feb.	25-26
"	13	Fast of Esther	Saturday*	March	10
"	14-15	Purim	Sun.-Mon.	"	11-12
Nissan.		Rosh-Chodesh	Tuesday	"	27
"	15	First Day of Passover	Tuesday	Apr.	10
Iyar.		Rosh-Chodesh	Wed.-Thurs.	"	25-26
"	18	Lag-B'Omer 33d day of Omer.	Sunday	May	13
Sivan	1	Rosh-Chodesh	Friday	"	25
"	6	First Day of Pentecost	Wednesday	"	30
Tammuz.		Rosh-Chodesh	Sat.-Sun.	June	23-24
"	17	Fast of Tammuz	Tuesday	July	10
Av	1	Rosh-Chodesh	Monday	"	23
"	9	Fast of Av	Tuesday	"	31
Ellul.		Rosh-Chodesh	Tues.-Wed.	Aug.	21-22

* Observed on previous Thursday.

EVENTFUL RECORDS.

A. M. 2982.—ABIJAH victorious against JEROBOHAM.

" 2983.—ASA, his son, succeeded to the kingdom, which he held for forty-one years.

" 2985.—JEROBOHAM 1ST, King of Israel, was succeeded by his son NADAB, who reigned two years.

" 2986.—NADAB was killed by BAASHA, who reigned twenty-four years.

" 2998.—ASA, King of Judah, obtained a victory over ZERAH, King of Ethiopia.

" 3009.—ELAH, son of BAASHA, King of Israel, succeeded his father, and reigned nearly two years.

		1906.			
Tishri	1	First Day of New Year..........	Thursday	Sept.	20
"	3	Fast of Gedaliah	Saturday*	"	22
"	10	Yom-Kippoor	Saturday	"	29
"	15	First Day of Tabernacle.........	Thursday	Oct.	4
"	21	Hoshannah-Rabbah..............	Wednesday	"	10
"	22	Sh'mini Atseres	Thursday	"	11
"	23	Simchas-Torah.................	Friday	"	12
Cheshvan.		Rosh-Chodesh	Fri.-Sat.	"	19-20
Kislev	1	Rosh-Chodesh	Sunday	Nov.	18
"	25	First Day of Chanukah........ ...	Wednesday	Dec.	12
Tebet.		Rosh-Chodesh	Mon.-Tues.	"	17-18
"	10	Fast of Tebet..................	Thursday	"	27
		1907.			
Sh'vat	1	Rosh-Chodesh....	Wednesday	Jan.	16
Adar.		Rosh-Chodesh	Thurs.-Fri.	Feb.	14-15
"	13	Fast of Esther.................	Wednesday	"	27
"	14-15	Purim......................	Thurs.-Fri.	{ " { March	28 1
Nissan	1	Rosh-Chodesh....	Saturday	"	16
"	15	First Day of Passover...........	Saturday	"	30
Iyar.		Rosh-Chodesh..................	Sun.-Mon.	Apr.	14-15
"	18	Lag-B'Omer.................. 33d day of Omer.	Thursday	May	2
Sivan	1	Rosh-Chodesh..	Tuesday	"	14
"	6	First Day of Pentecost..........	Sunday	"	19
Tammuz.		Rosh-Chodesh	Wed.-Thurs.	June	12-13
"	17	Fast of Tammuz....	Saturday*	"	29
Av.	-	Rosh-Chodesh....	Friday	July	12
"	9	Fast of Av....	Saturday*	"	20.
Ellul.		Rosh-Chodesh.................	Sat.-Sun.	Aug.	10-11

* Observed the day following.

EVENTFUL RECORDS.

A. M.   3010.—ELAH was killed by an officer of the household named ZIMRI, who only reigned seven days, but during this short usurpation murdered every male of BAASHA'S house. He was besieged in his palace by OMRI, captain of the host, and finding every chance of retreat cut off and no possibility of escape, he set fire to the palace and perished with it. OMRI was then made king, and reigned over twelve years.

"   3014.—A civil war took place between OMRI and TIBNI; on the death of the latter, OMRI was acknowledged king by the people.

34

People Noted for Intelligence and Thrift

are always patrons of the best of its kind. In other words, they know a good thing when they see it because it is a study with them which becomes second nature. This is one of the reasons why so many of the Jewish people are patrons of life insurance, for they early recognized its peculiar merits, and took advantage of its benefits.

It is also the reason why so many of the successful, shrewd business men among them are patrons and policy-holders with

The Hartford Life and Annuity Insurance Company
under its Safety Fund System,

which is unprecedented in the elements of ample security, equity of contract, and economy of cost.

THE SAFETY FUND SYSTEM is a plan of PURE INSURANCE. No investment feature is united with it, except that greatest and best of all financial investments, an indemnity that makes provision for a man's family in the event of his premature death.

Are you insured? If not, it will pay you to investigate this plan at once. If you are, it will pay you to carry a Policy under THE SAFETY FUND SYSTEM, because it is the best, and the best is always the cheapest.

$50.00 invested in a SAFETY FUND POLICY, will furnish as much indemnity as $100.00 invested in the old way.

Home Office of the Company: Hartford, Conn.

STEPHEN BALL, Secretary.   A. T. SMITH, Supt. Agencies.

1907.

Tishri	1	First Day of New Year	Monday	Sept.	9
"	3	Fast of Gedaliah	Wednesday	"	11
"	10	Yom-Kippoor....................	Wednesday	"	18
"	15	First Day of Tabernacle.........	Monday	"	23
"	21	Hoshannah-Rabbah.............	Sunday	"	29
"	22	Sh'mini-Atseres.................	Monday	"	30
"	23	Simchas-Torah..................	Tuesday	Oct.	1
Cheshvan.		Rosh-Chodesh....	Tues.-Wed.	"	8-9
Kislev	1	Rosh-Chodesh	Thursday	Nov.	7
"	25	First Day of Chanukah.	Sunday	Dec.	1
Tebet.		Rosh-Chodesh	Friday	"	6
"	10	Fast of Tebet..................	Sunday	"	15

1908.

Sh'vat	1	Rosh-Chodesh	Saturday	Jan.	4
Adar.		Rosh-Chodesh	Sun.-Mon.	Feb.	2-3
2d Adar.		Rosh-Chodesh	Tues.-Wed.	March	3-4
"	13	Fast of Esther....,.......... ...	Monday	"	16
"	14-15	Purim.........................	Tues.-Wed.	"	17-18
Nissan	1	Rosh-Chodesh	Thursday	April	2
"	15	First Day of Passover............	Thursday	"	16
Iyar.		Rosh-Chodesh	Fri.-Sat.	May	1-2
"	18	Lag-B'Omer.................... 33d day of Omer.	Tuesday	"	19
Sivan.		Rosh-Chodesh	Sunday	"	31
"	6	First Day of Pentecost..........	Friday	June	5
Tammuz.		Rosh-Chodesh	Mon.-Tues.	"	29-30
"	17	Fast of Tammuz...............	Thursday	July	16
Av.		Rosh-Chodesh....	Wednesday	"	29
"	9	Fast of Av....	Thursday	Aug.	6
Ellul.		Rosh-Chodesh	Thurs.-Fri.	"	27-28

EVENTFUL RECORDS.

A. M. 3021.—OMRI built Samaria. AHAB, his son, succeeded him and reigned twenty-two years.

" 3024.—ASA, King of Judah, was succeeded by his son JEHOSHAPHAT, who reigned twenty-five years, during which time the prophets ELIJAH and ELISHA existed.

" 3041.—OBADIAH prophesied. In a battle between AHAB and JEHOSHAPHAT, the former was fatally wounded. AHAZIAH, his son, reigned after him for two years.

" 3042.—The combined fleets of Judah and Israel were wrecked in an expedition to Tarshish.

1908.

Tishri	1	First Day of New Year	Saturday	Sept.	26
"	3	Fast of Gedaliah...............	Monday	"	28
"	10	Yom-Kippoor..................	Monday	Oct.	5
"	15	First Day of Tabernacle..........	Saturday	"	10
"	21	Hoshannah-Rabbah..............	Friday	"	16
"	22	Sh'mini-Atseres................	Saturday	"	17
"	23	Simchas-Torah..................	Sunday	"	18
Cheshvan.		Rosh-Chodesh	Sun.-Mon.	"	25-26
Kislev.		Rosh-Chodesh	Tues.-Wed.	Nov. 24-25	
"	25	First Day of Chanukah..	Saturday	Dec.	19
Tebet.		Rosh-Chodesh	Thurs.-Fri.	"	24-25

1909.

"	10	Fast of Tebet..................	Sunday	Jan.	3
Sh'vat.		Rosh-Chodesh	Saturday	"	23
Adar.		Rosh-Chodesh	Sun.-Mon.	Feb. 21-22	
"	13	Fast of Esther.................	Saturday*	Mar.	6
"	14-15	Purim......	Sun.-Mon.	"	7-8
Nissan	1	Rosh-Chodesh	Tuesday	"	23
"	15	First Day of Passover...........	Tuesday	Apr.	6
Iyar.		Rosh-Chodesh	Wed.-Thurs.	"	21 22
"	18	Lag-B'Omer	Sunday	May	9
		33d day of Omer.			
Sivan.		Rosh-Chodesh	Friday	"	21
"	6	First Day of Pentecost..........	Wednesday	"	26
Tammuz.		Rosh-Chodesh	Sat.-Sun.	June 19-20	
"	17	Fast of Tammuz	Tuesday	July	6
Av.		Rosh-Chodesh	Monday	"	19
"	9	Fast of Av....................	Tuesday	"	27
Ellul.		Rosh-Chodesh	Tues.-Wed.	Aug. 17-18	

* Observed Thursday previous.

EVENTFUL RECORDS.

A. M. 3043.—JORAM succeeded his brother AHAZIAH on the throne of Israel and reigned twelve years.

" 3047.—JEHOSHAPHAT united his son JEHORAM with him in the government, and reigned eight years. AHAZIAH succeeded his father to the kingdom of Judah, but after reigning one year was killed in a battle with JEHU, King of Israel.

" 3055.—Regal authority was assumed by his mother, ATHALIAH, who reigned six years. She destroyed all the members of the royal family, excepting an infant named JOASH. son of AHAZIAH, who was hidden in the Temple by his aunt, JEHOSHABETH, wife of JEHOIDA, the High Priest.

1909.

Tishri	1	First Day of New Year	Thursday	Sept.	16
"	3	Fast of Gedaliah...............	Saturday*	"	18
"	10	Yom-Kippoor..................	Saturday	"	25
"	15	First Day of Tabernacle..........	Thursday	"	30
"	21	Hoshannah-Rabbah..............	Wednesday	Oct.	6
"	22	Sh'mini-Atseres.................	Thursday	"	7
"	23	Simchas-Torah.................	Friday	"	8
Cheshvan.		Rosh-Chodesh	Fri -Sat.	"	15-16
Kislev.		Rosh-Chodesh	Sunday	Nov.	14
"	25	First Day of Chanukah	Wednesday	Dec.	8
Tebet.		Rosh-Chodesh	Monday	"	13
"	10	Fast of Tebet..................	Wednesday	"	22

1910.

Sh'vat	1	Rosh-Chodesh	Tuesday	Jan.	11
Adar.		Rosh-Chodesh	Wed.-Thurs.	Feb.	9-10
2d Adar.		Rosh-Chodesh	Fri.-Sat.	Mar.	11-12
"	13	Fast of Esther.................	Thursday	"	24
"	14-15	Purim........................	Fri.-Sat.	"	25-26
Nissan.		Rosh-Chodesh	Sunday	April	10
"	15	First Day of Passover	Sunday	"	24
Iyar.		Rosh-Chodesh	Mon.-Tues.	May	9
"	18	Lag-B'Omer.......	Friday	"	27
		33d day of Omer.			
Sivan.		Rosh-Chodesh	Wednesday	June	8
"	6	First Day of Pentecost...........	Monday	"	13
Tammuz.		Rosh-Chodesh	Thurs.-Fri	July	7-8
"	17	Fast of Tammuz................	Sunday	"	24
Av.		Rosh-Chodesh	Saturday	Aug.	6
"	9	Fast of Av....................	Sunday	"	14
Ellul.		Rosh-Chodesh	Sun.-Mon.	Sept.	4-5

* Observed the following day.

EVENTFUL RECORDS.

A. M. 3061.—Queen ATHALIAH killed by the populace, and JOASH declared king when only seven years old. JONAH prophesied during this reign.

" 3083.—JEOAHAZ succeeded his father, JEHU, to the kingdom of Israel, and reigned fifteen years

" 3098.—JEOASH. his son, next reigned for a period of sixteen years.

" 3100.—JOASH, King of Judah, ordered ZECHARIAH, the High Priest, to be stoned to death in the Temple He obtained peace from the King of Syria by purchase. and was slain in a conspiracy. AMAZIAH, his son, succeeded him, and reigned twenty nine years. HOSEA commenced to prophesy at this time.

		1910.			
Tishri	1	First Day of New Year..........	Tuesday	Oct.	4
"	3	Fast of Gedaliah	Thursday	"	6
"	10	Yom-Kippoor...................	Thursday	"	13
"	15	First Day of Tabernacle.........	Tuesday	"	18
"	21	Hoshannah-Rabbah.............	Monday	"	24
"	22	Sh'mini-Atseres................	Tuesday	"	25
"	23	Simchas-Torah.................	Wednesday	"	26
Cheshvan.		Rosh-Chodesh	Wed.-Thurs.	Nov.	2-3
Kislev	1	Rosh-Chodesh	Friday	Dec.	2
"	25	First Day of Chanukah`.........	Monday	"	26
Tebet.		Rosh-Chodesh	Sat.-Sun.	{ "	31
				1911	
		1911.		{ Jan.	1
"	10	Fast of Tebet..................	Tuesday	"	10
Sh'vat	1	Rosh-Chodesh	Monday	"	30
Adar.		Rosh-Chodesh	Tues.-Wed.	{ Feb.	28
				{ March	1
"	13	Fast of Esther.................	Monday	"	13
"	14-15	Purim ....:.............	Tues.-Wed.	"	14-15
Nissan	1	Rosh-Chodesh	Thursday	"	30
"	15	First Day of Passover...........	Thursday	Apr.	13
Iyar.		Rosh-Chodesh	Fri.-Sat.	"	28-29
"	18	Lag-B'Omer....................	Tuesday	May	16
		33d day of Omer.			
Sivan	1	Rosh-Chodesh	Sunday	"	28
"	6	First Day of Pentecost..........	Friday	June	2
Tammuz.		Rosh-Chodesh	Mon.-Tues.	"	26-27
"	17	Fast of Tammuz................	Thursday	July	13
Av	1	Rosh-Chodesh	Wednesday	"	26
"	9	Fast of Av	Thursday	Aug.	3
Ellul.		Rosh-Chodesh	Thurs.-Fri.	"	24-25

EVENTFUL RECORDS.

A. M. 3112.—A victory obtained over Edom by Amaziah.

" 3113.—Amaziah challenged Jeoash. King of Israel, who defeated him, took him prisoner, pillaged Jerusalem and the Temple.

" 3114.—Jeroboham II., son of Jeoash, succeeded to the kingdom of Israel, and reigned forty-one years.

" 3129.—Amaziah, who had been taken captive by Jeoash, was slain. His son, Uzziah, succeeded him and reigned fifty-two years. The term of his government is dated from 3115, as, although not actually king, he assumed royal authority in that year, when his father was conquered and made prisoner.

42

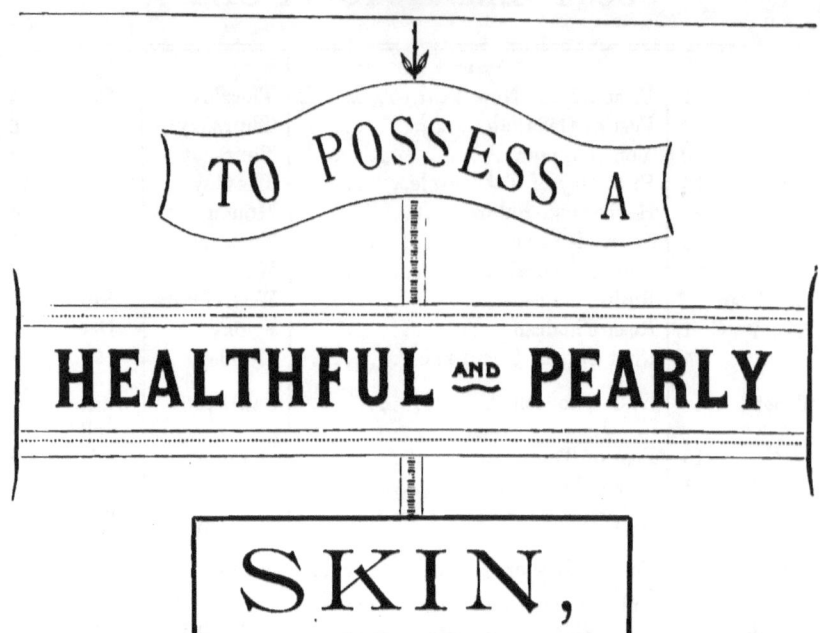

TO POSSESS A

HEALTHFUL AND PEARLY

SKIN,

- AND A -

CLEAR, UNBLEMISHED COMPLEXION,

BATHE WITH

GLENN'S SULPHUR SOAP

FOR A PURIFIER. Irrefragable evidence exists which proves conclusively that it produces the equally sure beneficial effects with the most popular and reliable sulphur bath, whether artificial or gushing from the bosom of Mother Nature. Rheumatic ailments as well as eruptive complaints, Sores, Pimples and Abrasions of the Skin, are speedily and entirely removed by it.

SOLD BY ALL DRUGGISTS.

		1911.			
Tishri	1	First Day of New Year..........	Saturday	Sept.	23
"	3	Fast of Gedaliah................	Monday	"	25
"	10	Yom-Kippoor	Monday	Oct.	2
"	15	First Day of Tabernacle	Saturday	"	7
"	21	Hoshannah-Rabbah	Friday	"	13
"	22	Sh'mini-Atseres................	Saturday	"	14
"	23	Simchas-Torah.................	Sunday	"	15
Cheshvan.		Rosh-Chodesh	Sun.-Mon.	"	22-23
Kislev.		Rosh-Chodesh	Tues.-Wed.	Nov.	22-23
"	25	First Day of Chanukah	Saturday	Dec.	16
Tebet.		Rosh-Chodesh	Thurs.-Fri..	"	21-22
"	10	Fast of Tebet..................	Sunday	"	31
		1912.			
Sh'vat	1	Rosh-Chodesh	Saturday	Jan.	20
Adar.		Rosh-Chodesh	Sun.-Mon.	Feb.	18-19
"	13	Fast of Esther.................	Saturday*	Mar.	2
"	14-15	Purim	Sun.-Mon.	"	3-4
Nissan	1	Rosh-Chodesh	Tuesday	"	19
"	15	First Day of Passover...........	Tuesday	April	2
Iyar.		Rosh-Chodesh	Wed.-Thurs.	"	17-18
"	18	Lag-B'Omer...................	Sunday	May	5
		33d day of Omer.			
Sivan	1	Rosh-Chodesh	Friday	"	17
"	6	First Day of Pentecost.	Wednesday	"	22
Tammuz.		Rosh-Chodesh	Sat.-Sun.	June	15-16
"	17	Fast of Tammuz...............	Tuesday	July	2
Av	1	Rosh-Chodesh	Monday	"	15
"	9	Fast of Av	Tuesday	"	23
Ellul.		Rosh-Chodesh	Tues.-Wed.	Aug.	13-14

* Observed on previous Thursday.

EVENTFUL RECORDS.

A. M. 3140.—Isaiah began to prophesy.

" 3154.—Zechariah succeeded his father, Jeroboham II., to the kingdom of Israel, but had not reigned more than six months when he was killed in a conspiracy headed by Shallum, who usurped the crown, but held it only one month, when he in turn was slain by Menahem, who reigned ten years. During this time, in order to obtain peace, he paid to Phul, King of Assyria, a thousand talents—about $600,000.

" 3160.—Micah prophesied.

		1912.			
Tishri	1	First Day of New Year..........	Thursday	Sept.	12
"	3	Fast of Gedaliah	Saturday*	"	14
"	10	Yom-Kippoor	Saturday	"	21
"	15	First Day of Tabernacle.........	Thursday	"	26
"	21	Hoshannah-Rabbah.............	Wednesday	Oct.	2
"	22	Sh'mini-Atseres	Thursday	"	3
"	23	Simchas-Torah.................	Friday	"	4
Cheshvan.		Rosh-Chodesh	Fri.-Sat.	"	11-12
Kislev.		Rosh-Chodesh	Sun. Mon.	Nov.	10-11
"	25	First Day of Chanukah..........	Thursday	Dec.	5
Tebet.		Rosh-Chodesh	Tues.-Wed.	"	10-11
"	10	Fast of Tebet..................	Friday	"	20
		1913.			
Sh'vat	1	Rosh-Chodesh....	Thursday	Jan.	9
1st Adar.		Rosh-Chodesh	Fri.-Sat.	Feb.	7-8
2d Adar.		Rosh-Chodesh.................	Sun.-Mon	Mar.	9-10
"	13	Fast of Esther.................	Saturday†	"	22
" 14-15		Purim.........................	Sun.-Mon.	"	23-24
Nissan	1	Rosh-Chodesh....	Tuesday	Apr.	8
"	15	First Day of Passover...........	Tuesday	"	22
Iyar.		Rosh-Chodesh.................	Wed.-Thurs.	May	7-8
"	18	Lag-B'Omer...................	Sunday	"	25
		33d day of Omer.			
Sivan	1	Rosh-Chodesh..	Friday	June	6
"	6	First Day of Pentecost..........	Wednesday	"	11
Tammuz.		Rosh-Chodesh	Sat.-Sun.	July	5-6
"	17	Fast of Tammuz....	Tuesday	"	22
Av	1	Rosh-Chodesh....	Monday	Aug.	4
"	9	Fast of Av....	Tuesday	"	12
Ellul.		Rosh-Chodesh.................	Tues.-Wed.	Sept.	2-3

* Observed following day.   † Observed Thursday previous.

EVENTFUL RECORDS.

A. M.   3165.—MENAHEM, King of Israel, was succeeded by his son PEKAIAH, who reigned two years, when he was conspired against and assassinated by PEKAH, a usurper, who reigned for twenty years.

"   3168.—UZZIAH, King of Judah, succeeded in 3184 by his son JOTHAM, who reigned sixteen years, when he was followed by his son AHAZ, who also reigned sixteen years.

"   3186.—In the second year of the reign of AHAZ, he defeated RESIN, King of Syria, and PEKAH, King of Israel, who had attacked him.

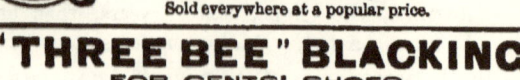

		1913.			
Tishri	1	First Day of New Year	Thursday	Oct.	2
"	3	Fast of Gedaliah	Saturday*	"	4
"	10	Yom-Kippoor	Saturday	"	11
"	15	First Day of Tabernacle	Thursday	"	16
"	21	Hoshannah-Rabbah	Wednesday	"	22
"	22	Sh'mini-Atseres	Thursday	"	23
"	23	Simchas-Torah	Friday	"	24
Cheshvan.		Rosh-Chodesh	Fri.-Sat.	{ "	31
				{ Nov.	1
Kislev.		Rosh-Chodesh	Sunday	"	30
"	25	First Day of Chanukah.	Wednesday	Dec.	24
Tebet.		Rosh-Chodesh	Mon.-Tues.	"	29-30
		1914.			
"	10	Fast of Tebet	Thursday	Jan.	8
Sh'vat	1	Rosh-Chodesh	Wednesday	"	28
Adar.		Rosh-Chodesh	Thurs. Fri.	Feb.	26-27
"	13	Fast of Esther	Wednesday	"	11
"	14-15	Purim	Thurs.-Fri.	"	12-13
Nissan.		Rosh-Chodesh	Saturday	March	28
"	15	First Day of Passover	Saturday	April	11
Iyar.		Rosh-Chodesh	Sun.-Mon.	"	26-27
"	18	Lag-B'Omer. 33d day of Omer.	Thursday	May	14
Sivan.		Rosh-Chodesh	Tuesday	"	26
"	6	First Day of Pentecost	Sunday	"	31
Tammuz.		Rosh-Chodesh	Wed.-Thurs.	June	24-25
"	17	Fast of Tammuz	Saturday*	July	11
Av.		Rosh-Chodesh	Friday	"	24
"	9	Fast of Av	Saturday*	Aug.	1
Ellul.		Rosh-Chodesh	Sat.-Sun.	"	22-23

* Observed day following.

EVENTFUL RECORDS.

A. M. 3187. —AHAZ formed an alliance with NINUS the Younger, successor to SARDANAPALUS, who is called in the scriptures TIGLATH-PILESER. TIGLATH-PILESER fought against RESIN and killed him, taking as prisoners the tribes of Reuben, Gad, and half of Manasseh. .

" 3188.—HOSEA murdered PEKAH and attempted to gain the crown of the kingdom of Israel; but there being other aspirants for its possession, anarchy and a civil war ensued.

" 3190.—The prophet JOEL lived.

1914.

Tishri	1	First Day of New Year	Monday	Sept.	21
"	3	Fast of Gedaliah................	Wednesday	"	23
"	10	Yom-Kippoor...................	Wednesday	"	30
"	15	First Day of Tabernacle.........	Monday	Oct.	5
"	21	Hoshannah-Rabbah..............	Sunday	"	11
"	22	Sh'mini-Atseres.................	Monday	"	12
"	23	Simchas-Torah..................	Tuesday	"	13
Cheshvan.		Rosh-Chodesh	Tues.-Wed.	"	20-21
Kislev	1	Rosh-Chodesh	Thursday	Nov.	19
"	25	First Day of Chanukah	Sunday	Dec.	13
Tebet	1	Rosh-Chodesh	Friday	"	18
"	10	Fast of Tebet....................	Sunday	"	27

1915.

Sh'vat	1	Rosh-Chodesh	Saturday	Jan.	16
Adar.		Rosh-Chodesh	Sun.-Mon.	Feb. 14-15	
"	13	Fast of Esther..................	Saturday*	"	27
"	14-15	Purim........................	Sun.-Mon.	{ "	28
				{ Mar.	1
Nissan	1	Rosh-Chodesh	Tuesday	"	16
"	15	First Day of Passover	Tuesday	"	30
Iyar.		Rosh-Chodesh	Wed.-Thurs.	Apr. 14-15	
"	18	Lag-B'Omer........	Sunday	May	2
		33d day of Omer.			
Sivan	1	Rosh-Chodesh	Friday	"	14
"	6	First Day of Pentecost..........	Wednesday	"	19
Tammuz.		Rosh-Chodesh	Sat.-Sun.	June 12-13	
"	17	Fast of Tammuz................	Tuesday	"	29
Av	1	Rosh-Chodesh	Monday	July	12
"	9	Fast of Av....................	Tuesday	"	20
Ellul.		Rosh-Chodesh	Tues.-Wed.	Aug. 10-11	

* Observed on Thursday previous.

EVENTFUL RECORDS.

A. M. 3196.—After eight years' warfare, HOSEA became king and reigned for nine years.

" 3198.—He formed an alliance with So, King of Egypt, against SAL-MANAZAR, the successor of TIGLATH-PILESER, but they were unsuccessful.

" 3199.—AHAZ, King of Judah, was succeeded by his son HEZEKIAH, who reigned twenty-nine years.

" 3202.—After a lapse of four years, HOSEA again revolted, and siege was laid to Samaria.

		1915.			
Tishri	1	First Day of New Year	Thursday	Sept.	9
"	3	Fast of Gedaliah...............	Saturday*	"	11
"	10	Yom-Kippoor..................	Saturday	"	18
"	15	First Day of Tabernacle.........	Thursday	"	23
"	21	Hoshannah-Rabbah.............	Wednesday	"	29
"	22	Sh'mini-Atseres...............	Thursday	"	30
"	23	Simchas-Torah.................	Friday	Oct.	1
Cheshvan.		Rosh-Chodesh	Fri.-Sat.	"	8-9
Kislev.		Rosh-Chodesh	Sun.-Mon.	Nov.	7-8
"	25	First Day of Chanukah.........	Thursday	Dec.	2
Tebet.		Rosh-Chodesh	Tues.-Wed.	"	7-8
"	10	Fast of Tebet.................	Friday	"	17
		1916.			
Sh'vat	1	Rosh-Chodesh	Thursday	Jan.	6
Adar.		Rosh-Chodesh	Fri.-Sat.	Feb.	4-5
2d Adar.		Rosh-Chodesh	Sun.-Mon.	Mar.	5-6
"	13	Fast of Esther.................	Saturday†	"	18
"	14-15	Purim......	Sun.-Mon.	"	19 20
Nissan	1	Rosh-Chodesh	Tuesday	Apr.	4
"	15	First Day of Passover...........	Tuesday	"	18
Iyar.		Rosh-Chodesh	Wed.-Thurs.	May	3-4
"	18	Lag-B'Omer	Sunday	"	21
		33d day of Omer.			
Sivan	1	Rosh-Chodesh	Friday	June	2
"	6	First Day of Pentecost..........	Wednesday	"	7
Tammuz.		Rosh-Chodesh	Sat.-Sun.	July	1-2
"	17	Fast of Tammuz	Tuesday	"	18
Av	1	Rosh-Chodesh	Monday	"	31
"	9	Fast of Av....................	Tuesday	Aug.	8
Ellul.		Rosh-Chodesh	Tues.-Wed.	"	29-30

* Observed following day.   † Observed Thursday previous.

EVENTFUL RECORDS.

A. M.   3205.—Samaria was taken after three years' siege, and the remainder of the ten tribes made captives. This terminated the kingdom of Israel.

About this time it is said that some Jews migrated to Germany and settled there.   It is also mentioned by Don ISAAC ABARBANEL that during the time of the first Temple there were families of his name residing at Seville and Valencia; from which it may be inferred that, in consequence of the unsettled and disturbed condition of Judea at that time, some of the people removed from it.

Illinois Springfield Watches.

"Illinois" Watches, manufactured by the Illinois Watch Company, Springfield, Illinois, are the Most Reliable Time-keepers on the market.

Manufactured in all grades and sizes.

Every Illinois Watch is warranted by the Company. Send for our Illustrated Catalogue.

Springfield, Illinois.

11 John Street, New York.   104 State Street, Chicago.

220 Sutter Street, San Francisco.

The "Opera" Piano Warerooms

Are among the finest in the City. A large assortment of the "OPERA" UPRIGHT PIANOS always on hand. New styles, fancy and plain woods. Prices are consistent with good workmanship.

Special Terms to Responsible Parties.

— PRICES EXTREMELY MODERATE. —

Every Instrument Warranted Five Years.

PEEK & SON, 212 to 216 West 47th Street,

Corner Broadway, New York.

		1916.			
Tishri	1	First Day of New Year	Thursday	Sept.	28
"	3	Fast of Gedaliah	Saturday*	"	30
"	10	Yom-Kippoor...................	Saturday	Oct.	7
"	15	First Day of Tabernacle..........	Thursday	"	12
"	21	Hoshannah-Rabbah..............	Wednesday	"	18
"	22	Sh'mini-Atseres................	Thursday	"	19
"	23	Simchas-Torah.................	Friday	"	20
Cheshvan.		Rosh-Chodesh	Fri.-Sat.	"	27-28
Kislev	1	Rosh-Chodesh	Sunday	Nov.	26
"	25	First Day of Chanukah	Wednesday	Dec.	20
Tebet.		Rosh-Chodesh	Mon.-Tues.	"	25-26
		1917.			
"	10	Fast of Tebet..................	Thursday	Jan.	4
Sh'vat	1	Rosh-Chodesh	Wednesday	"	24
Adar.		Rosh-Chodesh	Thurs.-Fri.	Feb.	22-23
"	13	Fast of Esther................	Wednesday	March	7
"	14-15	Purim	Thurs.-Fri.	"	8-9
Nissan	1	Rosh-Chodesh	Saturday	"	24
"	15	First Day of Passover	Saturday	April	7
Iyar.		Rosh-Chodesh	Sun.-Mon.	"	22-23
"	18	Lag-B'Omer...................	Thursday	May	10
		33d day of Omer.			
Sivan	1	Rosh-Chodesh	Tuesday	"	22
"	6	First Day of Pentecost..........	Sunday	"	27
Tammuz.		Rosh-Chodesh	Wed.-Thurs.	June	20-21
"	17	Fast of Tammuz................	Saturday*	July	7
Av	1	Rosh-Chodesh	Friday	"	20
"	9	Fast of Av	Saturday*	"	28
Ellul.		Rosh-Chodesh	Sat.-Sun.	Aug.	18-19

* Observed following day.

EVENTFUL RECORDS.

A. M. 3212.—HEZEKIAH, King of Judah, being desirous of exempting himself from further payment of the tribute which the Assyrians had levied upon his kingdom in the time of his father, AHAZ, formed alliances with the Kings of Egypt and Ethiopia. SENNACHERIB, King of Assyria, went out against him, and he was only enabled to purchase peace by sacrificing many of the treasures of the Temple.

" 3213.—SENNACHERIB, encouraged by his success, renewed his march against Jerusalem, but was repulsed with the great loss of 185,000 men, and was slain by his own sons after his return to Nineveh.

		1917.			
Tishri	1	First Day of New Year	Monday	Sept.	17
"	3	Fast of Gedaliah	Wednesday	"	19
"	10	Yom-Kippoor	Wednesday	"	26
"	15	First Day of Tabernacle	Monday	Oct.	1
"	21	Hoshannah-Rabbah	Sunday	"	7
"	22	Sh'mini-Atseres................	Monday	"	8
"	23	Simchas-Torah..................	Tuesday	"	9
Cheshvan.		Rosh-Chodesh	Tues.-Wed.	"	16-17
Kislev.		Rosh-Chodesh	Thurs.-Fri.	Nov.	15-16
"	25	First Day of Chanukah	Monday	Dec.	10
Tebet.		Rosh-Chodesh	Sat.-Sun.	"	15-16
"	10	Fast of Tebet..................	Tuesday	"	25
		1918.			
Sh'vat	1	Rosh-Chodesh	Monday	Jan.	14
Adar.		Rosh-Chodesh	Tues.-Wed.	Feb.	12-13
"	13	Fast of Esther.................	Monday	"	25
"	14-15	Purim	Tues.-Wed.	"	26-27
Nissan.		Rosh-Chodesh	Thursday	Mar.	14
"	15	First Day of Passover...........	Thursday	"	28
Iyar.		Rosh-Chodesh	Fri. Sat.	Apr.	12-13
"	18	Lag-B'Omer...................	Tuesday	"	30
		33d day of Omer.			
Sivan	1	Rosh-Chodesh........	Sunday	May	12
"	6	First Day of Pentecost.	Friday	"	17
Tammuz.		Rosh-Chodesh	Mon.-Tues.	June	10-11
"	17	Fast of Tammuz	Thursday	"	27
Av	1	Rosh-Chodesh	Wednesday	July	10
"	9	Fast of Av	Thursday	"	18
Ellul.		Rosh-Chodesh	Thurs.-Fri.	Aug.	8-9

EVENTFUL RECORDS.

A. M. 3214.—SENNACHERIB was succeeded by ASSARDON, otherwise called BALADAN.

" 3224.—HEZEKIAH's sickness and recovery. The Sun said to have gone back ten degrees (2 Kings xx., 9–11).

" 3226.—MERODACH-BALADAN, the successor of ASSARDON, sent ambassadors to HEZEKIAH to congratulate him on his recovery. He exhibited to them his great treasures, as a result of which act ISAIAH foretold the Babylonian captivity.

" 3228.—HEZEKIAH was succeeded by his son MANASSEH, who reigned the long term of fifty-five years.

56

		1918.			
Tishri	1	First Day of New Year..........	Saturday	Sept.	7
"	3	Fast of Gedaliah	Monday	"	9
"	10	Yom-Kippoor	Monday	"	16
"	15	First Day of Tabernacle.........	Saturday	"	21
"	21	Hoshannah-Rabbah..............	Friday	"	27
"	22	Sh'mini Atseres	Saturday	"	28
"	23	Simchas-Torah.	Sunday	"	29
Cheshvan.		Rosh-Chodesh	Sun.-Mon.	Oct.	6-7
Kislev	1	Rosh-Chodesh	Tuesday	Nov.	5
"	25	First Day of Chanukah..........	Friday	"	29
Tebet	1	Rosh-Chodesh	Wednesday	Dec.	4
"	10	Fast of Tebet.................	Friday	"	.13
		1919.			
Sh'vat.		Rosh-Chodesh.................	Thursday	Jan.	2
Adar.		Rosh-Chodesh	Fri.-Sat.	{ .. Feb.	31 1
2d Adar.		Rosh-Chodesh.................	Sun.-Mon.	Mar.	2-3
"	13	Fast of Esther.................	Saturday*	"	15
"	14-15	Purim.........................	Sun. Mon.	"	16-17
Nissan	1	Rosh-Chodesh.................	Tuesday	April	1
"	15	First Day of Passover...........	Tuesday	"	15
Iyar.		Rosh-Chodesh.................	Wed.-Thurs.	{ " May	30 1
"	18	Lag-B'Omer.................... 33d day of Omer.	Sunday	"	18
Sivan	1	Rosh-Chodesh..................	Friday	"	30
"	6	First Day of Pentecost..........	Wednesday	June	4
Tammuz.		Rosh-Chodesh	Sat.-Sun.	"	28-29
"	17	Fast of Tammuz....	Tuesday	July	15
Av	1	Rosh-Chodesh....	Monday	"	28
"	9	Fast of Av....	Tuesday	Aug.	5
Ellul.		Rosh-Chodesh.................	Tues.-Wed.	"	26-27

* Observed Thursday previous.

EVENTFUL RECORDS.

A. M. 3240.—NAHUM prophesied.

" 3249.—MANASSEH made captive and taken to Babylon.

" 3250.—Having repented of his evil doings, he prayed for pardon and was restored to his kingdom. His prayer is found in the Apocrypha.

" 3254.—HABAKKUK, the prophet, lived.

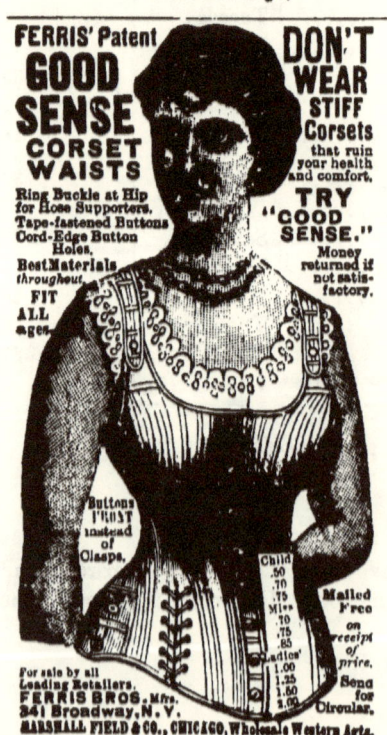

1919.

Tishri	1	First Day of New Year	Thursday	Sept.	25
"	3	Fast of Gedaliah	Saturday*	"	27
"	10	Yom-Kippoor	Saturday	Oct.	4
"	15	First Day of Tabernacle..........	Thursday	"	9
"	21	Hoshannah-Rabbah.............	Wednesday	"	15
"	22	Sh'mini-Atseres................	Thursday	"	16
"	23	Simchas-Torah.................	Friday	"	17
Cheshvan.		Rosh-Chodesh....	Fri.-Sat.	"	24-25
Kislev	1	Rosh-Chodesh	Sunday	Nov.	23
"	25	First Day of Chanukah..........	Wednesday	Dec.	17
Tebet.		Rosh-Chodesh	Mon.-Tues.	"	22-23

1920.

"	10	Fast of Tebet..................	Thursday	Jan.	1
Sh'vat	1	Rosh-Chodesh	Wednesday	"	21
Adar.		Rosh-Chodesh	Thurs.-Fri.	Feb.	19-20
"	13	Fast of Esther............... ...	Wednesday	Mar.	3
"	14-15	Purim.........................	Thurs.-Fri.	"	4-5
Nissan	1	Rosh-Chodesh	Saturday	"	20
"	15	First Day of Passover...........	Saturday	Apr.	3
Iyar.		Rosh-Chodesh	Sun.-Mon.	"	18-19
"	18	Lag-B'Omer...................	Thursday	May	6
		33d day of Omer.			
Sivan	1	Rosh-Chodesh	Tuesday	"	18
"	6	First Day of Pentecost..........	Sunday	"	23
Tammuz.		Rosh-Chodesh	Wed.-Thurs.	June	16-17
"	17	Fast of Tammuz...............	Saturday*	July	3
Av	1	Rosh-Chodesh....	Friday	"	16
"	9	Fast of Av....	Saturday*	"	24
Ellul.		Rosh-Chodesh	Sat.-Sun..	Aug.	14-15

* Observed following day.

EVENTFUL RECORDS.

A. M. 3283.—AMON succeeded his father, MANASSEH, but only reigned two years, being killed by a conspiracy.

" 3285.—He was succeeded by his son JOSIAH, who reigned thirty-one years.

" 3292.—JOSIAH removed many abuses and restored the practice of divine worship, which, during the two preceding reigns, had been greatly neglected and interrupted.

" 3298.—The prophecies of JEREMIAH commenced.

" 3302.—A book of the Law was discovered in the Temple by HILKIAH, the High Priest.

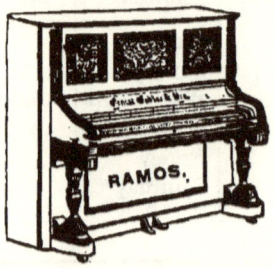

1920.

Tishri	1	First Day of New Year	Monday	Sept. 13
"	3	Fast of Gedaliah................	Wednesday	" 15
"	10	Yom-Kippoor...................	Wednesday	" 22
"	15	First Day of Tabernacle.........	Monday	" 27
"	21	Hoshannah-Rabbah..............	Sunday	Oct. 3
"	22	Sh'mini-Atseres.................	Monday	" 4
"	23	Simchas-Torah..................	Tuesday	" 5
Cheshvan.		Rosh-Chodesh	Tues -Wed.	" 12-13
Kislev.		Rosh-Chodesh	Thurs.-Fri.	Nov. 11-12
"	25	First Day of Chanukah	Monday	Dec. 6
Tebet.		Rosh-Chodesh	Sat.-Sun.	" 11-12
"	10	Fast of Tebet..................	Tuesday	" 21

1921.

Sh'vat	1	Rosh-Chodesh	Monday	Jan. 10
Adar.		Rosh-Chodesh	Tues.-Wed.	Feb. 8-9
2d Adar.		Rosh-Chodesh	Thurs -Fri.	Mar. 10-11
"	13	Fast of Esther..................	Wednesday	" 23
"	14-15	Purim.........................	Thurs.-Fri.	" 24-25
Nissan	1	Rosh-Chodesh	Saturday	April 9
"	15	First Day of Passover	Saturday	" 23
Iyar.		Rosh-Chodesh	Sun.-Mon.	May 8-9
"	18	Lag-B'Omer	Thursday	" 26
		33d day of Omer.		
Sivan	1	Rosh-Chodesh	Tuesday	June 7
"	6	First Day of Pentecost............	Sunday	" 12
Tammuz.		Rosh-Chodesh	Wed.-Thurs.	July 6-7
"	17	Fast of Tammuz................	Saturday*	" 23
Av	1	Rosh-Chodesh ....,........	Friday	Aug. 5
"	9	Fast of Av.....................	Saturday*	" 13
Ellul.		Rosh-Chodesh	Sat.-Sun.	Sept. 3-4

* Observed day following.

EVENTFUL RECORDS.

A. M. 3303.—The feast of Passover was celebrated with unparalleled solemnity and grandeur.

ZEPHANIAH prophesied.

" 3316.—In a battle against PHARAOH-NECHO, JOSIAH was wounded. He returned to Jerusalem and died there. His son JEOACHAZ succeeded him, and three months afterwards PHARAOH-NECHO imposed a tax on the country of two talents of silver and one of gold (about $100,000), deposed JEOACHAZ, and gave the throne to his brother, JEHOIAKIM, who reigned eleven years.

		1921.			
Tishri	1	First Day of New Year	Monday	Oct.	3
"	3	Fast of Gedaliah..............	Wednesday	"	5
"	10	Yom-Kippoor.................	Wednesday	"	12
"	15	First Day of Tabernacle.........	Monday	"	17
"	21	Hoshannah-Rabbah.............	Sunday	"	23
"	22	Sh'mini-Atseres..............	Monday	"	24
"	23	Simchas-Torah................	Tuesday	"	25
Cheshvan.		Rosh-Chodesh	Tues -Wed.	Nov.	1-2
Kislev.		Rosh-Chodesh	Thurs.-Fri.	Dec.	1-2
"	25	First Day of Chanukah..........	Monday	"	26
		1922.		"	31
Tebet.		Rosh-Chodesh	Sat.-Sun.	1922 Jan.	1
"	10	Fast of Tebet.................	Tuesday	"	10
Sh'vat	1	Rosh-Chodesh	Monday	"	30
Adar.		Rosh-Chodesh	Tues.-Wed.	Feb. Mar.	28 1
"	13	Fast of Esther.................	Monday	"	13
"	14-15	Purim......	Tues.-Wed.	"	14 15
Nissan	1	Rosh-Chodesh	Thursday	"	30
"	15	First Day of Passover...........	Thursday	Apr.	13
Iyar.		Rosh-Chodesh	Fri.-Sat.	"	28-29
"	18	Lag-B'Omer .... 33d day of Omer.	Tuesday	May	16
Sivan	1	Rosh-Chodesh	Sunday	"	28
"	6	First Day of Pentecost..........	Friday	June	2
Tammuz.		Rosh-Chodesh	Mon.-Tues.	"	26-27
"	17	Fast of Tammuz	Thursday	July	13
Av	1	Rosh-Chodesh	Wednesday	"	26
"	9	Fast of Av....................	Thursday	Aug.	3
Ellul.		Rosh-Chodesh	Thurs.-Fri.	"	24-25

EVENTFUL RECORDS.

A. M. 3319.—JEHOIAKIM became tributary to NEBUCHADNEZZAR. DANIEL and many noted men were led into captivity.

" 3323.—A revolt by JEHOIAKIM quelled by NEBUCHADNEZZAR, and the Temple plundered by him.

" 3327.—JEHOIAKIM put to death, was succeeded by his eight-year-old son JEHOIACHIN, whom NEBUCHADNEZZAR sent for to Babylon and placed in prison. The throne was given to his uncle, ZEDEKIAH, who reigned eleven years, and was the last King of Judah.

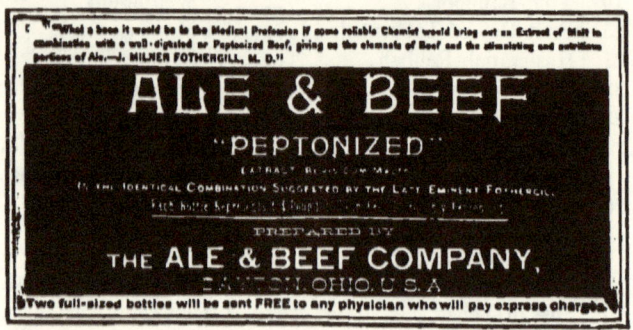

		1922.			
Tishri	1	First Day of New Year	Saturday	Sept.	23
"	3	Fast of Gedaliah	Monday	"	25
"	10	Yom-Kippoor...................	Monday ·	Oct.	2
"	15	First Day of Tabernacle.........	Saturday	"	7
"	21	Hoshaunah-Rabbah..............	Friday	"	13
"	22	Sh'mini-Atseres................	Saturday	"	14
"	23	Simchas-Torah.................	Sunday	"	15
Cheshvan.		Rosh-Chodesh	Sun.-Mon.	"	22-23
Kislev	1	Rosh-Chodesh	Tuesday	Nov.	21
"	25	First Day of Chanukah	Friday	Dec.	15
Tebet	1	Rosh-Chodesh	Wednesday	"	20
"	10	Fast of Tebet...................	Friday	"	29
		1923.			
Sh'vat	1	Rosh-Chodesh	Thursday	Jan.	18
Adar.		Rosh-Chodesh	Fri.-Sat.	Feb.	16-17
"	13	Fast of Esther.................	Thursday	Mar.	1
"	14-15	Purim	Fri.-Sat.	"	2-3
Nissan	1	Rosh-Chodesh	Sunday	"	18
"	15	First Day of Passover	Sunday	April	1
Iyar.		Rosh-Chodesh	Mon.-Tues.	"	16-17
"	18	Lag-B'Omer................... 33d day of Omer.	Friday	May	4
Sivan	1	Rosh-Chodesh	Wednesday	"	16
"	6	First Day of Pentecost..........	Monday	"	21
Tammuz.		Rosh-Chodesh	Thurs.-Fri.	June 14-15	
"	17	Fast of Tammuz................	Sunday	July	1
Av	1	Rosh-Chodesh	Saturday	"	14
"	9	Fast of Av	Sunday	"	22
Ellul.		Rosh-Chodesh	Sun.-Mon	Aug. 12-13	

EVENTFUL RECORDS.

A. M. 3332.—The prophecies of EZEKIEL commenced.

" 3336.—ZEDEKIAH revolted against Babylon's oppression. On the tenth day of the month of *Tebet*, NEBUCHADNEZZAR laid siege to Jerusalem.

" 3338.—On the ninth day of *Av* he took the city, burned the Temple, massacred many of the people, caused the sons of ZEDEKIAH to be killed in their father's presence, then had his eyes put out, and took him and a large number of prisoners captive into Babylon. This ended the kingdom of Judah, after it had been in existence four hundred and fifty-four years. under David and his lineal descendants.

		1923.			
Tishri	1	First Day of New Year..........	Tuesday	Sept.	11
"	3	Fast of Gedaliah	Thursday	"	13
"	10	Yom-Kippoor	Thursday	"	20
"	15	First Day of Tabernacle	Tuesday	"	25
"	21	Hoshaunah-Rabbah	Monday	Oct.	1
"	22	Sh'mini-Atseres.................	Tuesday	"	2
"	23	Simchas-Torah..................	Wednesday	"	3
Cheshvan.		Rosh-Chodesh	Wed.-Thur.	"	10-11
Kislev	1	Rosh-Chodesh	Friday	Nov.	9
"	25	First Day of Chanukah	Monday	Dec.	3
Tebet.		Rosh Chodesh	Sat.-Sun.	"	8-9
"	10	Fast of Tebet...................	Tuesday	"	18
		1924.			
Sh'vat	1	Rosh-Chodesh	Monday	Jan.	7
Adar.		Rosh-Chodesh	Tues.-Wed.	Feb.	5-6
2d Adar.		Rosh-Chodesh..................	Thurs -Fri.	Mar.	6-7
"	13	Fast of Esther.................	Wednesday	"	19
"	14-15	Purim	Thurs.-Fri.	"	20-21
Nissan	1	Rosh-Chodesh	Saturday	Apr.	5
"	15	First Day of Passover...........	Saturday	"	19
Iyar.		Rosh-Chodesh	Sun.-Mon.	May	4-5
"	18	Lag-B'Omer...................	Thursday	"	22
		33d day of Omer.			
Sivan	1	Rosh Chodesh .... ,..	Tuesday	June	3
"	6	First Day of Pentecost.	Sunday	"	8
Tammuz.		Rosh Chodesh	Wed.-Thur.	July	2-3
"	17	Fast of Tammuz	Saturday*	"	19
Av	1	Rosh-Chodesh	Friday	Aug.	1
"	9	Fast of Av	Saturday*	"	9
Ellul.		Rosh-Chodesh	Sat.-Sun.	"	30-31

* Observed on following day.

EVENTFUL RECORDS.

A. M. 3339.—NEBUCHADNEZZAR appointed GEDALIAH, son of AHIKAM, Governor of Judea. He was murdered on the third day of *Tishri.*

" 3363.—SHADRACH, MESHACH, and ABEDNEGO, the three companions of DANIEL, were cast into a furnace because they refused to become apostates.

" 3364.—The throne of Babylon occupied by EVIL-MERODACH. JEHOI-ACHIN, who had been imprisoned for thirty-seven years, was released by him, and a generous provision allowed for his maintenance.

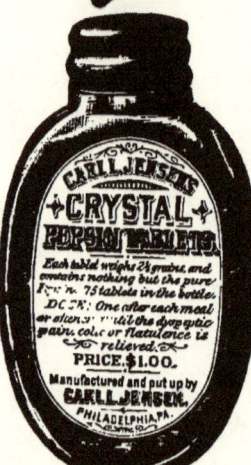

		1924.			
Tishri	1	First Day of New Year..........	Monday	Sept.	29
"	3	Fast of Gedaliah................	Wednesday	Oct.	1
"	10	Yom-Kippoor	Wednesday	"	8
"	15	First Day of Tabernacle	Monday	"	13
"	21	Hoshannah-Rabbah	Sunday	"	19
"	22	Sh'mini-Atseres.................	Monday	"	20
"	23	Simchas-Torah	Tuesday	"	21
Cheshvan.		Rosh-Chodesh	Tues.-Wed.	"	28-29
Kislev.		Rosh-Chodesh	Thurs.-Fri.	Nov.	27-28
"	25	First Day of Chanukah	Monday	Dec.	22
Tebet.		Rosh-Chodesh	Sat.-Sun.	"	27-28
		1925.			
"	10	Fast of Tebet	Tuesday	Jan.	6
Sh'vat	1	Rosh-Chodesh	Monday	"	26
Adar.		Rosh-Chodesh	Tues.-Wed.	Feb.	24-25
"	13	Fast of Esther.................	Monday	Mar.	9
"	14-15	Purim	Tues.-Wed.	"	10-11
Nissan	1	Rosh-Chodesh	Thursday	"	26
"	15	First Day of Passover	Thursday	Apr.	9
Iyar.		Rosh-Chodesh	Fri.-Sat.	"	24-25
"	18	Lag-B'Omer................... 33d day of Omer.	Tuesday	May	12
Sivan	1	Rosh-Chodesh	Sunday	"	24
"	6	First Day of Pentecost	Friday	"	29
Tammuz.		Rosh-Chodesh	Mon.-Tues.	June	22-23
"	17	Fast of Tammuz................	Thursday	July	9
Av	1	Rosh-Chodesh	Wednesday	"	22
"	9	Fast of Av	Thursday	"	30
Ellul.		Rosh-Chodesh	Thurs.-Fri.	Aug.	20-21

EVENTFUL RECORDS.

A. M. 3389.—The impious feast of BELSHAZZAR, and his death.
DANIEL refused to worship an idol and was thrown into a den of lions. He had prophesied at Babylon during the reign of its three preceding kings.

" 3390.—CYRUS became sovereign. He conquered DARIUS, directed the Jews to return to Jerusalem and rebuild the Temple, and aided and protected them whilst they were doing so.

" 3393.—ARTAXERXES, called in the Bible AHASUERUS, killed and succeeded CYRUS.

" 3396.—ESTHER, cousin of the pious MORDECAI, and who, being an orphan, had been adopted by him, was chosen by King AHASUERUS as his wife, and thereby became Queen of all Media and Persia.

		1925.			
Tishri	1	First Day of New Year	Saturday	Sept.	19
"	3	Fast of Gedaliah................	Monday	"	21
"	10	Yom-Kippoor	Monday	"	28
"	15	First Day of Tabernacle	Saturday	Oct.	3
"	21	Hoshannah-Rabbah	Friday	"	9
"	22	Sh'mini-Atseres..........	Saturday	"	10
"	23	Simchas-Torah	Sunday	"	11
Cheshvan.		Rosh-Chodesh	Sun.-Mon.	"	18-19
Kislev.	·	Rosh-Chodesh	Tues.-Wed.	Nov.	17-18
"	25	First Day of Chanukah	Saturday	Dec.	12
Tebet.		Rosh-Chodesh	Thurs.-Fri.	"	17-18
"	10	Fast of Tebet	Sunday	"	27
		1926.			
Sh'vat	1	Rosh-Chodesh	Saturday	Jan.	16
Adar.		Rosh-Chodesh	Sun.-Mon.	Feb.	14-15
"	13	Fast of Esther............:......	Saturday*	"	27
"	14-15	Purim	Sun.-Mon.	{ "	28
				{ Mar.	1
Nissan	1	Rosh-Chodesh	Tuesday	"	16
"	15	First Day of Passover	Tuesday	"	30
Iyar.		Rosh-Chodesh	Wed.-Thurs.	Apr.	14-15
"	18	Lag-B'Omer.....................	Sunday	May	2
		33d day of Omer.			
Sivan	1	Rosh-Chodesh	Friday	"	14
"	6	First Day of Pentecost	Wednesday	"	19
Tammuz.		Rosh-Chodesh	Sat.-Sun.	June	12-13
"	17	Fast of Tammuz................	Tuesday	"	29
Av	1	Rosh-Chodesh	Monday	July	12
"	9	Fast of Av	Tuesday	"	20
Ellul.		Rosh-Chodesh	Tues.-Wed.	Aug.	10-11

* Observed Thursday previous.

EVENTFUL RECORDS.

A. M.   3404.—She interceded with the king against the infernal machinations of HAMAN and saved her people from destruction, in commemoration of which the festival of *Purim* was instituted.

"   3408.—HAGGAI, ZECHARIAH, and MALACHI prophesied. and the building of the second Temple. at Jerusalem, was begun.

"   3412.—It was completed and dedicated on the twenty-third day of the month *Adar*.

"   3413.—EZRA, the prophet and scribe, left Babylon and went to Jerusalem.

5687 A.M. 1926-'27 C.Æ.

		1926.			
Tishri	1	First Day of New Year	Thursday	Sept.	9
"	3	Fast of Gedaliah.................	Saturday*	"	11
"	10	Yom-Kippoor....................	Saturday	"	18
"	15	First Day of Tabernacle..........	Thursday	"	23
"	21	Hoshannah-Rabbah..............	Wednesday	"	29
"	22	Sh'mini-Atseres................	Thursday	"	30
"	23	Simchas-Torah.................	Friday	Oct.	1
Cheshvan.		Rosh-Chodesh	Fri.·Sat.	"	8-9
Kislev	1	Rosh-Chodesh	Sunday	Nov.	7
"	25	First Day of Chanukah	Wednesday	Dec.	1
Tebet	1	Rosh-Chodesh	Monday	"	6
"	10	Fast of Tebet..........·........	Wednesday	"	15
		1927.			
Sh'vat	1	Rosh-Chodesh	Tuesday	Jan.	4
Adar.		Rosh-Chodesh	Wed.-Thurs.	Feb.	2-3
2d Adar.		Rosh-Chodesh	Fri.-Sat.	Mar.	4-5
"	13	Fast of Esther.................	Thursday	"	17
"	14-15	Purim.......................	Fri.-Sat.	"	18-19
Nissan	1	Rosh-Chodesh	Sunday	April	3
"	15	First Day of Passover	Sunday	"	17
Iyar.		Rosh-Chodesh	Mon.-Tues.	May	2-3
"	18	Lag-B'Omer .... 33d day of Omer.	Friday	"	20
Sivan	1	Rosh-Chodesh	Wednesday	June.	1
"	6	First Day of Pentecost...........	Monday	"	6-7
Tammuz.		Rosh·Chodesh	Thurs.-Fri.	" July	30 1
"	17	Fast of Tammuz...............	Sunday	"	17
Av	1	Rosh-Chodesh	Saturday	"	30
"	9	Fast of Av......·.............	Sunday	Aug.	7
Ellul.		Rosh-Chodesh .. '.............	Sun.-Mon.	"	28-29

* Observed on following day.

EVENTFUL RECORDS.

A. M. 3426.—NEHEMIAH had the city walls rebuilt.

" 3448.—The Temple was visited by ALEXANDER THE GREAT, who offered sacrifice therein.

" 3457.—One hundred thousand Jewish captives carried into Egypt by PTOLEMY, who conquered Judea.

" 3463.—They were taken from him by ANTIGONUS.

74

		1927.			
Tishri	1	First Day of New Year	Tuesday	Sept.	27
"	3	Fast of Gedaliah	Thursday	"	29
"	10	Yom-Kippoor.	Thursday	Oct.	6
"	15	First Day of Tabernacle.	Tuesday	"	11
"	21	Hoshannah-Rabbah	Monday	"	17
"	22	Sh'mini-Atseres	Tuesday	"	18
"	23	Simchas-Torah.	Wednesday	"	19
Cheshvan.		Rosh-Chodesh	Wed.-Thurs.	"	26-27
Kislev	1	Rosh-Chodesh	Friday	Nov.	25
"	25	First Day of Chanukah	Monday	Dec.	19
Tebet.		Rosh-Chodesh.	Sat.-Sun.	"	24-25
		1928.			
"	10	Fast of Tebet	Tuesday	Jan.	3
Sh'vat	1	Rosh-Chodesh	Monday	"	23
Adar.		Rosh-Chodesh	Tues.-Wed.	Feb.	21-22
"	13	Fast of Esther	Monday	Mar.	5
"	14-15	Purim.	Tues.-Wed.	"	6-7
Nissan	1	Rosh-Chodesh	Thursday	"	22
"	15	First Day of Passover	Thursday	Apr.	5
Iyar.		Rosh-Chodesh	Fri.-Sat.	"	20-21
"	18	Lag-B'Omer	Tuesday	May	8
		33d day of Omer.			
Sivan	1	Rosh-Chodesh	Sunday	"	20
"	6	First Day of Pentecost	Friday	"	25
Tammuz.		Rosh-Chodesh	Mon.-Tues.	Jun.	18-19
"	17	Fast of Tammuz	Thursday	July	5
Av	1	Rosh-Chodesh	Wednesday	"	18
"	9	Fast of Av	Thursday	"	26
Ellul.		Rosh-Chodesh	Thurs.-Fri.	Aug.	2-3

EVENTFUL RECORDS.

A. M. 3465.—PTOLEMY retook the prisoners. The Syrians swarmed the
country and exacted contributions, but PTOLEMY ultimately
gained possession of it.

" 3516.—The Jews were granted the same privileges by ANTIOCHUS THE
GREAT as were enjoyed by his other subjects.
Seventy most learned men of the Jews were called upon by
PTOLEMY PHILADELPHUS to make a translation of the holy
books into the Greek language, the cost of which is said to
have been not less than $350,000.

" 3560.—An attempt was made by PTOLEMY PHILOPATER to enter
the sanctuary of the Holy Temple by force. Prevented
from doing so, he avenged himself by killing sixty thousand
Jews on his return to Egypt.

		1928.			
Tishri	1	First Day of New Year..........	Saturday	Sept.	15
"	3	Fast of Gedaliah	Monday	"	17
"	10	Yom-Kippoor	Monday	"	24
"	15	First Day of Tabernacle	Saturday	"	29
"	21	Hoshannah-Rabbah	Friday	Oct.	5
"	22	Sh'mini-Atseres.................	Saturday	"	6
"	23	Simchas-Torah..................	Sunday	"	7
Cheshvan.		Rosh-Chodesh	Sun.-Mon.	"	14-15
Kislev.		Rosh-Chodesh	Tues.-Wed.	Nov.	13-14
"	25	First Day of Chanukah	Saturday	Dec.	8
Tebet.		Rosh-Chodesh	Thurs.-Fri.	"	13-14
"	10	Fast of Tebet..................	Sunday	"	23
		1929.			
Sh'vat	1	Rosh-Chodesh ...., ..	Saturday	Jan.	12
Adar.		Rosh-Chodesh	Sun.-Mon.	Feb.	10-11
2d Adar.		Rosh-Chodesh..................	Tues.-Wed.	Mar.	12-13
"	13	Fast of Esther.................	Monday	"	25
"	14-15	Purim	Tues.-Wed.	"	26-27
Nissan	1	Rosh-Chodesh	Thursday	Apr.	11
"	15	First Day of Passover...........	Thursday	"	25
Iyar.		Rosh-Chodesh	Fri.-Sat.	May	10-11
"	18	Lag-B'Omer...................	Tuesday	"	28
		33d day of Omer.			
Sivan	1	Rosh-Chodesh...........	Sunday	June	9
"	6	First Day of Pentecost.	Friday	"	14
Tammuz.		Rosh Chodesh	Mon.-Tues.	July	8-9
"	17	Fast of Tammuz	Thursday	"	25
Av	1	Rosh-Chodesh	Wednesday	Aug.	7
"	9	Fast of Av	Thursday	"	15
Ellul.		Rosh-Chodesh	Thurs.-Fri.	Sept.	5-6

EVENTFUL RECORDS.

A. M. 3616.—The Temple was pillaged and polluted by ANTIOCHUS EPI-
PHANES, who ordered a swine to be sacrificed on the altar.
He also forbade the observance of the Sabbath, festivals, and
the rite of circumcision.

" 3621.—MATTATHIAS, son of JOHANAN, the High Priest, who was the
first of the Asmonean dynasty, organized a revolt which terminated successfully. On their banners were inscribed the
words, *"Mee K'moucho B'Ileem Adonai,"* signifying,
"Who amongst the mighty is like unto thee, O Lord?"
The initials of these words forming the word MACBEE, he
and his descendants were called MACCABEES.

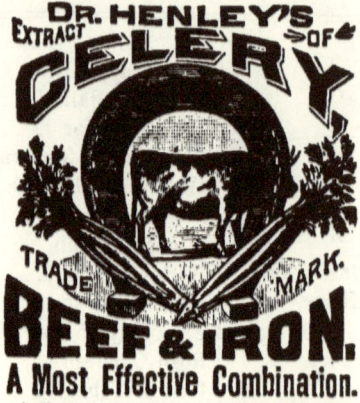
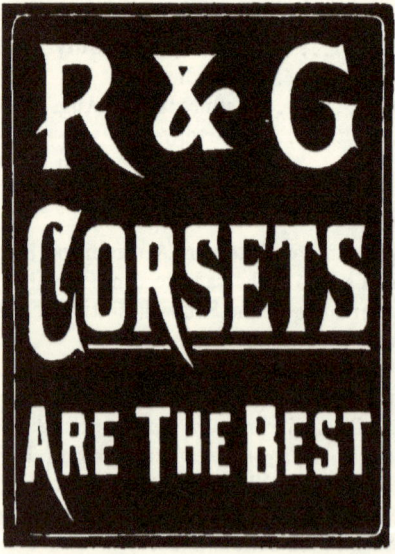

		1929.			
Tishri	1	First Day of New Year...........	Saturday	Oct.	5
"	3	Fast of Gedaliah	Monday	"	7
"	10	Yom-Kippoor...................	Monday	"	14
"	15	First Day of Tabernacle.........	Saturday	"	19
"	21	Hoshannah-Rabbah.............	Friday	"	25
"	22	Sh'mini-Atseres................	Saturday	"	26
"	23	Simchas-Torah.................	Sunday	"	27
Cheshvan.		Rosh-Chodesh	Sun.-Mon.	Nov.	3-4
Kislev	1	Rosh-Chodesh	Tuesday	Dec.	3
"	25	First Day of Chanukah	Friday	"	27
		1930.			
Tebet	1	Rosh-Chodesh	Wednesday	Jan.	1
"	10	Fast of Tebet..................	Friday	"	10
Sh'vat	1	Rosh-Chodesh	Thursday	"	30
Adar.		Rosh-Chodesh	Fri.-Sat.	{ Feb.	28
				{ Mar.	1
"	13	Fast of Esther.................	Thursday	"	13
"	14-15	Purim	Fri.-Sat.	"	14-15
Nissan	1	Rosh-Chodesh	Sunday	"	30
"	15	First Day of Passover	Sunday	April	13
Iyar.		Rosh-Chodesh ......,.........	Mon.-Tues.	"	28
"	18	Lag-B'Omer...................	Friday	May	16
		33d day of Omer.			
Sivan	1	Rosh-Chodesh	Wednesday	"	28
"	6	First Day of Pentecost..........	Monday	June	2
Tammuz.		Rosh-Chodesh	Thurs.-Fri.	"	26-27
"	17	Fast of Tammuz................	Sunday	July	13
Av	1	Rosh-Chodesh	Saturday	"	26
"	9	Fast of Av	Sunday	Aug.	3
Ellul.		Rosh-Chodesh	Sun.-Mon.	"	24-25

EVENTFUL RECORDS.

A. M. 3622.—MATTATHIAS died and was succeeded by his son JUDAH. who completely routed the Syrian army and slew many of its officers, including APOLLONIUS, its general-in-chief.

On regaining possession of the Temple, he purified and re-dedicated it, and resumed divine worship on the 25th day of *Kislev;* in commemoration of which the festival of CHANUKAH is celebrated. A treaty of alliance was effected with the Senate at Rome, ambassadors having been sent there for that purpose. A copy of the treaty was engraved on brazen tablets.

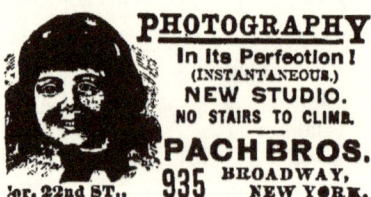

		1930.			
Tishri	1	First Day of New Year..........	Tuesday	Sept.	23
"	3	Fast of Gedaliah	Thursday	"	25
"	10	Yom-Kippoor	Thursday	Oct.	2
"	15	First Day of Tabernacle........	Tuesday	"	7
"	21	Hoshannah-Rabbah.............	Monday	"	13
"	22	Sh'mini Atseres	Tuesday	"	14
"	23	Simchas-Torah.	Wednesday	"	15
Cheshvan.		Rosh-Chodesh	Wed.-Thurs.	"	22-23
Kislev	1	Rosh-Chodesh	Friday	Nov.	21
"	25	First Day of Chanukah..........	Monday	Dec.	15
Tebet.		Rosh-Chodesh	Sat.-Sun.	"	20-21
"	10	Fast of Tebet..................	Tuesday	"	30
		1931.			
Sh'vat	1	Rosh-Chodesh	Monday	Jan.	19
Adar.		Rosh-Chodesh..................	Tues.-Wed.	Feb.	17-18
"	13	Fast of Esther.................	Monday	Mar.	2
"	14-15	Purim.........................	Tues.-Wed.	"	3-4
Nissan	1	Rosh-Chodesh....	Thursday	"	19
"	15	First Day of Passover...........	Thursday	April	2
Iyar.		Rosh-Chodesh..................	Fri.-Sat.	"	17-18
"	18	Lag-B'Omer................... 33d day of Omer.	Tuesday	May	5
Sivan	1	Rosh-Chodesh..	Sunday	"	17
"	6	First Day of Pentecost..........	Friday	"	22
Tammuz.		Rosh-Chodesh	Mon.-Tues.	June	15-16
"	17	Fast of Tammuz....	Thursday	July	2
Av	1	Rosh-Chodesh....	Wednesday	"	11
"	9	Fast of Av....	Thursday	"	19
Ellul.		Rosh-Chodesh.................	Thurs.-Fri.	Aug.	13-14

EVENTFUL RECORDS.

A. M. 3628.—JUDAH, having been deserted by some of his troops. was killed in battle against DEMETRIUS, whose forces were led by BAC-CHIDES and ALCIMUS. He was succeeded by his brother JONATHAN, who renewed the friendly relations with Rome and Lacedæmon.

" 3633.—TRYPHON treacherously seized JONATHAN and demanded a heavy ransom for his release, but killed him after the amount had been paid.

" 3634.—JONATHAN was succeeded by his brother SIMEON, and all the allies of Rome were favorably addressed on behalf of the Jews by the Consul LUCIUS.

		1931.			
Tishri	1	First Day of New Year	Saturday	Sept.	12
"	3	Fast of Gedaliah	Monday	"	14
"	10	Yom-Kippoor....................	Monday	"	21
"	15	First Day of Tabernacle..........	Saturday	"	2?
"	21	Hoshannah-Rabbah	Friday	Oct.	2
"	22	Sh'mini-Atseres.................	Saturday	"	3
"	23	Simchas-Torah..................	Sunday	"	4
Cheshvan.		Rosh-Chodesh....	Sun.-Mon.	"	11-1?
Kislev.		Rosh-Chodesh ....:...........	Tues.-Wed.	Nov.	10-1?
"	18	First Day of Chanukah..........	Saturday	Dec.	?
Tebet.		Rosh-Chodesh	Thurs.-Fri.	"	10-11
"	10	Fast of Tebet..................	Sunday	"	20
		1932.			
Sh'vat	1	Rosh-Chodesh	Saturday	Jan.	9
Adar.		Rosh-Chodesh	Sun.-Mon.	Feb.	7-8
2d Adar.		Rosh-Chodesh	Tues.-Wed.	Mar.	8 9
"	13	Fast of Esther................	Monday	"	21
"	14-15	Purim........................	Tues.-Wed.	"	22-23
Nissan	1	Rosh-Chodesh	Thursday	Apr.	7
"	15	First Day of Passover...........	Thursday	"	21
Iyar.		Rosh-Chodesh	Fri.-Sat.	May	6-7
"	18	Lag-B'Omer...................	Tuesday	"	24
		33d day of Omer.			
Sivan	1	Rosh-Chodesh	Sunday	June	5
"	6	First Day of Pentecost..........	Friday	"	10
Tammuz.		Rosh-Chodesh	Mon.-Tues.	July	4-5
"	17	Fast of Tammuz................	Thursday	"	21
Av	1	Rosh-Chodesh....	Wednesday	Aug.	3
"	9	Fast of Av....	Thursday	"	11
Ellul.		Rosh-Chodesh	Thurs.-Fri.	Sept.	1-2

EVENTFUL RECORDS.

A. M. 3642.—PTOLEMY, King of Egypt, and the son-in-law of SIMEON, assassinated the latter and his two sons at a feast. His object in doing so was to obtain the government of Judea, which he coveted. JOHN HYRCANUS, another son, managed to escape. On hearing of the cruel murder of his relatives, he waged war against PTOLEMY and drove him to take refuge in the castle of DAGON. Finding himself besieged there, unable to escape and having in his power his enemy's mother and brothers, he had them taken on to the battlements of the tower and cruelly tortured in JOHN's sight, threatening to throw his mother from the walls if he did not abandon the siege. She heroically encouraged and advised her son to the contrary, and suffered a martyr's death in the cause.

IS THE

ORIGINAL and ONLY PREPARATION of RAW FOOD.

A MOST WONDERFUL NUTRIENT
AND RESTORATIVE.

The vital principles of Beef concentrated. A highly condensed Raw Food Extract. Acceptable to the most delicate taste and smell. Retained by irritable stomachs that reject all other foods. It assimilates more readily than any other food known to the medical profession. Bovinine under the microscope shows the blood corpuscles in their normal condition strongly marked, while in other foods or extracts this vitally important element is destroyed by the action of heat in cooking.

Creates New and Vitalized Blood faster than any other preparation. Builds up the system after severe surgical operations. Soothes and alleviates ulcerated and cancerous conditions of the digestive organs.

Nursing Mothers, Infants and Children thrive surprisingly by its use.

" During the last four months of his sickness, the principal food of my father, General Grant, was Bovinine and milk; and it was the use of this incomparable food alone that enabled him to finish the second volume of his personal memoirs."

" OCTOBER 1st, 1885." "FRED. D. GRANT."

Carefully prepared from the formula of the late James P. Bush, by the J. P. Bush Mfg. Co., 44 Third Ave., Chicago, Ills.

Put up in 6 and 12 oz. sizes, at 60 cents and $1.00 per bottle.
TWELVE OUNCES CONTAIN THE STRENGTH OF TEN POUNDS OF MEAT.

PRINCIPAL OFFICE, 2 BARCLAY ST.(Astor House), N.Y.
FOR SALE BY ALL DRUGGISTS.

REBECCA AT THE WELL.

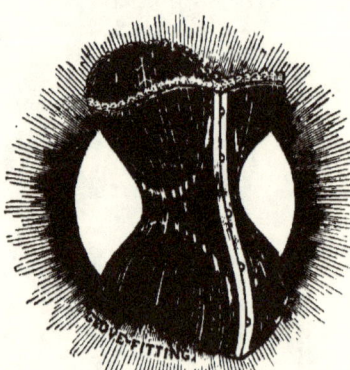

		1932.			
Tishri	1	First Day of New Year	Saturday	Oct.	1
"	3	Fast of Gedaliah	Monday	"	3
"	10	Yom-Kippoor	Monday	"	10
"	15	First Day of Tabernacle	Saturday	"	15
"	21	Hoshannah-Rabbah	Friday	"	21
"	22	Sh'mini-Atseres	Saturday	"	22
"	23	Simchas-Torah	Sunday	"	23
Cheshvan.		Rosh-Chodesh	Sun.-Mon.	"	30-31
Kislev.		Rosh-Chodesh	Tues.-Wed.	Nov.	29-30
"	25	First Day of Chanukah	Saturday	Dec.	24
Tebet.		Rosh-Chodesh	Thurs.-Fri.	"	29-30
		1933.			
"	10	Fast of Tebet	Sunday	Jan.	8
Sh'vat	1	Rosh-Chodesh	Saturday	"	28
Adar.		Rosh-Chodesh	Sun. Mon.	Feb.	26-27
"	13	Fast of Esther	Saturday*	Mar.	11
"	14-15	Purim	Sun.-Mon.	"	12-13
Nissan	1	Rosh-Chodesh	Tuesday	"	28
"	15	First Day of Passover	Tuesday	Apr.	11
Iyar.		Rosh-Chodesh	Wed.-Thurs.	"	26-27
"	18	Lag-B'Omer 33d day of Omer.	Sunday	May	14
Sivan	1	Rosh-Chodesh	Friday	"	26
"	6	First Day of Pentecost	Wednesday	"	31
Tammuz.		Rosh-Chodesh	Sat.-Sun.	June	24-25
"	17	Fast of Tammuz	Tuesday	July	11
Av	1	Rosh-Chodesh	Monday	"	24
"	9	Fast of Av	Tuesday	Aug.	1
Ellul.		Rosh-Chodesh	Tues.-Wed.	"	22-23

* Observed on Thursday previous

EVENTFUL RECORDS.

A. M. 3642.—ANTIOCHUS SIDETES besieged the Temple, but granted a truce of eight days to celebrate the Tabernacle feast, and even sent offerings thereto. This action produced peace and a treaty of alliance.

" 3648.—The commencement in Judea of Roman authority.

" 3665.—The government assumed by ARISTOBULUS, who had his mother and brother murdered.

" 3666.—His brother ALEXANDER succeeded him.

" 3667.—ALEXANDER engaged in war with PTOLEMY LATHYRUS and lost 30,000 men in an engagement.

		·1933.			
Tishri	1	First Day of New Year	Thursday	Sept.	21
"	3	Fast of Gedaliah..............	Saturday*	"	23
"	10	Yom-Kippoor..................	Saturday	"	30
"	15	First Day of Tabernacle.........	Thursday	Oct.	5
"	21	Hoshannah-Rabbah..............	Wednesday	"	11
"	22	Sh'mini-Atseres................	Thursday	"	12
"	23	Simches-Torah.................	Friday	"	13
Cheshvan.		Rosh-Chodesh	Fri.-Sat.	"	20-21
Kislev	1	Rosh-Chodesh	Sunday	Nov.	19
"	25	First Day of Chanukah..........	Wednesday	Dec.	13
Tebet.		Rosh Chodesh	Mon -Tues.	"	18-19
"	10	Fast of Tebet.	Thursday	"	28
		1934.			
Sh'vat	1	Rosh-Chodesh	Wednesday	Jan.	17
Adar.		Rosh-Chodesh	Thurs.-Fri.	Feb.	15-16
"	13	Fast of Esther	Wednesday	"	28
"	14-15	Purim	Thurs.-Fri.	Mar.	1-2
Nissan	1	Rosh-Chodesh	Saturday	"	17
"	15	First Day of Passover...........	Saturday	"	31
Iyar.		Rosh-Chodesh	Sun.-Mon.	Apr.	15-16
"	18	Lag-B'Omer................... 33d day of Omer.	Thursday	May	3
Sivan	1	Rosh-Chodesh	Tuesday	"	15
"	6	First Day of Pentecost...........	Sunday	"	20
Tammuz.		Rosh-Chodesh	Wed.-Thurs.	June	13-14
"	17	Fast of Tammuz	Saturday*	"	30
Av	1	Rosh-Chodesh	Friday	July	13
"	9	Fast of Av	Saturday*	"	21
Ellul.		Rosh-Chodesh	Sat.-Sun.	Aug.	11-12

* Observed following day.

EVENTFUL RECORDS.

A. M. 3669.—ALEXANDER afterwards formed an alliance with CLEOPATRA.

" 3674.—On the day of *Hoshannah-Rabbah*, the people having revolted, they violently assaulted ALEXANDER with their citrons, in retaliation for which, six thousand of the unarmed populace were killed by his troops.

" 3685.—Queen ALEXANDRA, his widow, acted as regent after his death.

" 3694.—Her two sons, ARISTOBULUS and HYRCANUS, disputed as to the succession, but came to an agreement by which ARISTOBULUS, the younger, was acknowledged.

		1934.			
Tishri	1	First Day of New Year.........	Monday	Sept	10
"	3	Fast of Gedaliah...............	Wednesday	"	12
"	10	Yom-Kippoor	Wednesday	"	19
"	15	First Day of Tabernacle	Monday	"	24
"	21	Hoshannah-Rabbah	Sunday	"	30
"	22	Sh'mini-Atseres................	Monday	Oct.	1
"	23	Simchas-Torah	Tuesday	"	2
Cheshvan.		Rosh-Chodesh	Tues.-Wed.	"	9-10
Kislev	1	Rosh-Chodesh	Thursday	Nov.	8
"	25	First Day of Chanukah	Sunday	Dec.	2
Tebet	1	Rosh-Chodesh	Friday	"	7
"	10	Fast of Tebet	Sunday	"	16
		1935.			
Sh'vat	1	Rosh-Chodesh	Saturday	Jan.	5
Adar.		Rosh-Chodesh	Sun.-Mon.	Feb.	3-4
2d Adar.		Rosh-Chodesh....	Tues -Wed.	Mar.	5-6
"	13	Fast of Esther.................	Monday	"	18
"	14-15	Purim	Tues.-Wed.	"	19-20
Nissan	1	Rosh-Chodesh	Thursday	Apr.	4
"	15	First Day of Passover	Thursday	"	18
Iyar.		Rosh-Chodesh	Fri.-Sat.	May	3-4
"	18	Lag-B'Omer...................	Tuesday	"	21
		33d day of Omer.			
Sivan	1	Rosh-Chodesh	Sunday	June	2
"	6	First Day of Pentecost	Friday	"	7
Tammuz.		Rosh-Chodesh	Mon.-Tues.	July	1-2
"	17	Fast of Tammuz................	Thursday	"	17
Av	1	Rosh-Chodesh	Wednesday	"	31
"	9	Fast of Av	Thursday	Aug.	8
Ellul.		Rosh-Chodesh	Thurs.-Fri.	"	29-20

EVENTFUL RECORDS.

A. M. 3699.—The two brothers were cited to appear before Pompey, and he, being dissatisfied with Aristobulus, deposed him and had him taken prisoner to Rome.

" 3700.—He then raised Hyrcanus to the throne, on condition of his paying a heavy tribute and not wearing a crown.

" 3713.—The Temple was pillaged and an enormous booty taken therefrom by Crassus.

" 3719.—The former alliance with the Romans was renewed with Julius Cæsar.

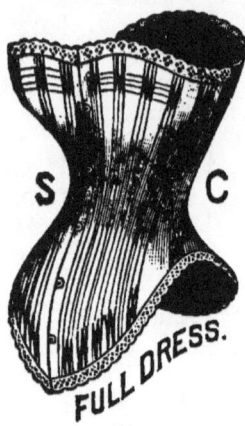
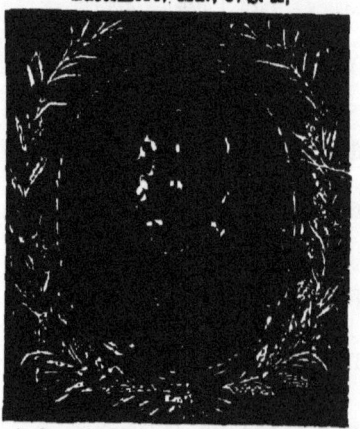

		1935.			
Tishri	1	First Day of New Year	Saturday	Sept.	28
"	3	Fast of Gedaliah...............	Monday	"	30
"	10	Yom-Kippoor	Monday	Oct.	7
"	15	First Day of Tabernacle	Saturday	"	12
"	21	Hoshannah-Rabbah	Friday	"	18
"	22	Sh'mini-Atseres..................	Saturday	"	19
"	23	Simchas-Torah	Sunday	"	20
Cheshvan.		Rosh-Chodesh	Sun.-Mon.	"	27-28
Kislev.		Rosh-Chodesh	Tues.-Wed.	Nov.	26-27
"	25	First Day of Chanukah	Saturday	Dec.	21
Tebet.		Rosh-Chodesh	Thurs.-Fri.	"	26-27
"	10	Fast of Tebet	Sunday	Jan.	5
Sh'vat	1	Rosh-Chodesh	Saturday	"	25
Adar.		Rosh-Chodesh	Sun.-Mon.	Feb.	23-24
"	13	Fast of Esther..................	Saturday*	Mar.	7
"	14-15	Purim	Sun.-Mon.	"	8-9
Nissan	1	Rosh-Chodesh	Tuesday	"	24
"	15	First Day of Passover	Tuesday	Apr.	7
Iyar.		Rosh-Chodesh	Wed.-Thurs.	"	22-23
"	18	Lag-B'Omer .... 33d day of Omer.	Sunday	May	10
Sivan	1	Rosh-Chodesh	Friday	"	22
"	6	First Day of Pentecost	Wednesday	"	27
Tammuz.		Rosh-Chodesh	Sat.-Sun.	June	20-21
"	17	Fast of Tammuz...............	Tuesday	July	7
Av	1	Rosh-Chodesh	Monday	"	20
"	9	Fast of Av	Tuesday	"	28
Ellul.		Rosh-Chodesh	Tues.-Wed.	Aug.	18-19

* Observed Thursday previous.

EVENTFUL RECORDS.

A. M. 3721.—On the death of JULIUS CÆSAR, all the requests of the Jews were granted by the Senate.

" 3722.—A contribution of seven hundred talents (about $400,000) was levied on Judea by CASSIUS.

" 3724.—The kingdom was now sought by ANTIGONUS, but HEROD and PHAZAEL, sons of ANTIPATER, were appointed Tetrarchs. ANTIGONUS was obliged to fly to Rome, and was granted the kingdom by the Senate.

" 3727.—The famous historian, JOSEPHUS, born.

		1936.			
Tishri	1	First Day of New Year	Thursday	Sept.	17
"	3	Fast of Gedaliah................	Saturday*	"	19
"	10	Yom-Kippoor..................	Saturday	"	26
"	15	First Day of Tabernacle.........	Thursday	Oct.	1
"	21	Hoshannah-Rabbah..............	Wednesday	"	7
"	22	Sh'mini-Atseres.................	Thursday	"	8
"	23	Simchas-Torah.................	Friday	"	9
Cheshvan.		Rosh-Chodesh	Fri. Sat.	"	16-17
Kislev	1	Rosh-Chodesh	Sunday	Nov.	15
"	25	First Day of Chanukah	Wednesday	Dec.	9
Tebet.		Rosh-Chodesh	Mon.-Tues.	"	14-15
"	10	Fast of Tebet..................	Thursday	"	24
		1937.			
Sh'vat	1	Rosh-Chodesh	Wednesday	Jan.	13
Adar.		Rosh-Chodesh	Thurs.-Fri.	Feb.	11-12
"	13	Fast of Esther.................	Wednesday	"	24
"	14-15	Purim..................	Thurs.-Fri.	"	25-26
Nissan	1	Rosh-Chodesh	Saturday	Mar.	13
"	15	First Day of Passover	Saturday	"	27
Iyar.		Rosh-Chodesh	Sun.-Mon.	Apr.	11-12
"	18	Lag-B'Omer	Thursday	"	29
		33d day of Omer.			
Sivan	1	Rosh-Chodesh	Tuesday	May	11
"	6	First Day of Pentecost...........	Sunday	"	16
Tammuz.		Rosh Chodesh	Wed.-Thur.	June	9-10
"	17	Fast of Tammuz................	Saturday*	"	26
Av	1	Rosh-Chodesh	Friday	July	9
"	9	Fast of Av....................	Saturday*	"	17
Ellul.		Rosh-Chodesh	Sat.-Sun.	Aug.	7-8

* Observed following day.

EVENTFUL RECORDS.

A. M.   3728.—The famous colleges of HILLEL and SHAMAI existed at this time.   They are noted as seats of learning where so many discussions were waged   The Chaldean paraphrases, known as the *Targum*, were written at this time by Rabbi JONATHAN. HEROD having returned and captured Jerusalem, ANTIGONUS was made prisoner and beheaded by MARC ANTONY.

"   3731.—HEROD and MARC ANTONY made common cause against AUGUSTUS CÆSAR.   A terrible famine existed throughout Judea, ten thousand men perishing in Jerusalem.

"   3742.—The rebuilding of the Temple was now begun.

"   3751.—The city of Cæsarea, built in honor of AUGUSTUS, was solemnly dedicated by HEROD.

		1937.			
Tishri	1	First Day of New Year	Monday	Sept.	6
"	3	Fast of Gedaliah	Wednesday	"	8
"	10	Yom-Kippoor..................	Wednesday	"	15
"	15	First Day of Tabernacle..........	Monday	"	20
"	21	Hoshannah-Rabbah..............	Sunday	"	26
"	22	Sh'mini-Atseres...............	Monday	"	27
"	23	Simchas-Torah...............	Tuesday	"	28
Cheshvan.		Rosh-Chodesh	Tues.-Wed.	Oct.	5-6
Kislev.		Rosh-Chodesh	Thurs.-Fri.	Nov.	4-5
"	25	First Day of Chanukah..........	Monday	"	28
Tebet.		Rosh-Chodesh..................	Sat.-Sun.	Dec.	4-5
"	10	Fast of Tebet..................	Tuesday	"	14
		1938.			
Sh'vat	1	Rosh-Chodesh	Monday	Jan.	3
Adar.		Rosh-Chodesh	Tues.-Wed.	Feb.	1-2
2d Adar.		Rosh-Chodesh	Thurs.-Fri.	Mar.	3-4
"	13	Fast of Esther................	Wednesday	"	16
"	14-15	Purim......	Thurs.-Fri.	"	17-18
Nissan	1	Rosh-Chodesh	Saturday	Apr.	2
"	15	First Day of Passover...........	Saturday	"	16
Iyar.		Rosh-Chodesh	Sun.-Mon.	May	1-2
"	18	Lag-B'Omer	Sunday	"	19
		33d day of Omer.			
Sivan	1	Rosh-Chodesh	Tuesday	"	31
"	6	First Day of Pentecost...	Sunday	June	5
Tammuz.		Rosh-Chodesh	Wed.-Thurs	"	29-30
"	17	Fast of Tammuz	Saturday*	July	16
Av	1	Rosh-Chodesh	Friday	"	29
"	9	Fast of Av....................	Saturday*	Aug.	6
Ellul.		Rosh-Chodesh	Sat.-Sun.	"	27-28

* Observed following day.

EVENTFUL RECORDS.

A. M.   3752.—To secure the valuable treasures which had been deposited in David's tomb, Herod ordered it to be opened. Two of his attendants were struck by lightning and killed whilst they were engaged in the act of desecration.

"   3757.—All former rights and privileges enjoyed by the Jews at Alexandria were ratified and confirmed by Augustus.

"   3760.—The Christian era now commenced, 1,312 years after the exodus of Israel from Egypt; and for the convenience of the general reader we shall from this point use that date.

		1938.			
Tishri	1	First Day of New Year	Monday	Sept.	26
"	3	Fast of Gedaliah	Wednesday	"	28
"	10	Yom-Kippoor	Wednesday	Oct.	5
"	15	First Day of Tabernacle	Monday	"	10
"	21	Hoshannah-Rabbah	Sunday	"	16
"	22	Sh'mini-Atseres	Monday	"	17
"	23	Simchas-Torah	Tuesday	"	18
Cheshvan.		Rosh-Chodesh	Tues.-Wed.	"	25-26
Kislev	1	Rosh-Chodesh	Thursday	Nov.	24
"	25	First Day of Chanukah	Sunday	Dec.	18
Tebet	1	Rosh-Chodesh	Friday	"	23
		1939.			
"	10	Fast of Tebet	Sunday	Jan.	1
Sh'vat	1	Rosh-Chodesh	Saturday	"	21
Adar.		Rosh-Chodesh	Sun.-Mon.	Feb.	19-20
"	13	Fast of Esther	Saturday *	Mar.	4
"	14-15	Purim	Sun.-Mon.	"	5-6
Nissan	1	Rosh-Chodesh	Tuesday	"	21
"	15	First Day of Passover	Tuesday	April	4
Iyar.		Rosh-Chodesh	Wed.-Thurs.	"	19-20
"	18	Lag-B'Omer	Sunday	May	7
		33d day of Omer.			
Sivan	1	Rosh-Chodesh	Friday	"	19
"	6	First Day of Pentecost	Wednesday	"	24
Tammuz.		Rosh-Chodesh	Sat.-Sun.	June	17-18
"	17	Fast of Tammuz	Tuesday	July	4
Av	1	Rosh-Chodesh	Monday	"	17
"	9	Fast of Av	Tuesday	"	25
Ellul.		Rosh-Chodesh	Tues.-Wed.	Aug.	15-16

* Observed Thursday previous.

EVENTFUL RECORDS.

C.Æ. 1.—HEROD was succeeded by his son ARCHELAUS.

" 10.—HEROD ANTIPAS succeeded to the government after his brother, ARCHELAUS.

" 15.—The edict in favor of the Jews, which had been issued by AUGUSTUS, was forwarded and proclaimed to the governors of every Roman province, including even Britain.

" 21.—Four impostors, in order to escape public punishment, fled from Judea to Rome. The misconduct of these fugitives was such in this latter city that the Jews residing there were ordered to quit.

5700 A.M.   1939-'40 C.Æ.

		1939.			
Tishri	1	First Day of New Year	Thursday	Sept.	14
"	3	Fast of Gedaliah	Saturday*	"	16
"	10	Yom-Kippoor	Saturday	"	23
"	15	First Day of Tabernacle	Thursday	"	28
"	21	Hoshannah-Rabbah	Wednesday	Oct.	4
"	22	Sh'mini-Atseres	Thursday	"	5
"	23	Simchas-Torah	Friday	"	6
Cheshvan.		Rosh-Chodesh	Fri.-Sat.	"	13-14
Kislev.		Rosh-Chodesh	Sun.-Mon.	Nov.	12-13
"	25	First Day of Chanukah	Thursday	Dec.	7
Tebet.		Rosh-Chodesh	Tues.-Wed.	"	12-13
"	10	Fast of Tebet	Friday	"	22
		1940.			
Sh'vat	1	Rosh-Chodesh	Thursday	Jan.	11
Adar.		Rosh-Chodesh	Fri.-Sat.	Feb.	9-10
2d Adar.		Rosh-Chodesh	Sun.-Mon.	Mar.	10-11
"	13	Fast of Esther	Saturday †	"	23
"	14-15	Purim	Sun.-Mon.	"	24-25
Nissan	1	Rosh-Chodesh	Tuesday	Apr.	9
"	15	First Day of Passover	Tuesday	"	23
Iyar.		Rosh-Chodesh	Wed.-Thurs.	May	8-9
"	18	Lag-B'Omer. 33d day of Omer.	Sunday	"	26
Sivan	1	Rosh-Chodesh	Friday	June	7
"	6	First Day of Pentecost	Wednesday	"	12
Tammuz.		Rosh-Chodesh	Sat.-Sun.	July	6-7
"	17	Fast of Tammuz	Tuesday	"	23
Av	1	Rosh-Chodesh	Monday	Aug.	5
"	9	Fast of Av	Tuesday	"	13
Ellul.		Rosh-Chodesh	Tues.-Wed.	Sept.	3-4

* Observed following day.   † Observed Thursday previous.

EVENTFUL RECORDS.

C.Æ.   21.—AGRIPPA succeeded his uncle, HEROD ANTIPAS.

"   28.—The seat of the Sanhedrin, hitherto held at Jerusalem, was removed to Jamnia.

"   36.—AGRIPPA took refuge in Rome, being obliged to flee from Jerusalem.

"   37.—TIBERIUS imprisoned him, but he was released in the following year.

"   40.—An order was issued by the Emperor CALIGULA that an image of himself should be placed in the Temple, but through the intercession of AGRIPPA the command was withdrawn.

		1940.			
Tishri	1	First Day of New Year...........	Thursday	Oct.	3
"	3	Fast of Gedaliah	Saturday*	"	5
"	10	Yom-Kippoor	Saturday	"	12
"	15	First Day of Tabernacle..........	Thursday	"	17
"	21	Hoshannah-Rabbah.............	Wednesday	"	23
"	22	Sh'mini-Atseres	Thursday	"	24
"	23	Simchas-Torah.................	Friday	"	25
Cheshvan.		Rosh-Chodesh	Fri.-Sat.	Nov.	1-2
Kislev	1	Rosh-Chodesh	Sunday	Dec.	1
"	25	First Day of Chanukah.........	Wednesday	"	25
Tebet.		Rosh-Chodesh	Mon.-Tues.	"	30-31
		1941.			
"	10	Fast of Tebet.................	Thursday	Jan.	9
Sh'vat	1	Rosh-Chodesh	Wednesday	"	29
Adar.		Rosh-Chodesh...............	Thurs.-Fri.	Feb.	27-28
"	13	Fast of Esther................	Wednesday	Mar.	12
"	14-15	Purim......................	Thurs.-Fri.	"	13-14
Nissan	1	Rosh-Chodesh....	Saturday	"	29
"	15	First Day of Passover..........	Saturday	April	12
Iyar.		Rosh-Chodesh...............	Sun.-Mon.	"	27-28
"	18	Lag-B'Omer..................	Thursday	May	15
		33d day of Omer.			
Sivan	1	Rosh-Chodesh..	Tuesday	"	27
"	6	First Day of Pentecost.........	Sunday	June	1
Tammuz.		Rosh-Chodesh	Wed.-Thurs.	"	25-26
"	17	Fast of Tammuz....	Saturday*	July	12
Av	1	Rosh-Chodesh....	Friday	"	25
"	9	Fast of Av....	Saturday*	Aug.	2
Ellul.		Rosh-Chodesh...............	Sat.-Sun.	"	23-24

* Observed following day.

EVENTFUL RECORDS.

C.Æ. 40.—A similar order having been issued to the Jews of Alexandria, they sent PHILO to appeal against it.

" 42.—There was an uprising in Alexandria against the Jews, and many were slain. PHILO went again to Rome in their behalf.

" 43.—PHILO returned, conveying a proclamation from CLAUDIUS, ratifying and according to them all the rights which AUGUSTUS had previously granted to them. This order was extended throughout the entire Roman Empire.

		1941.			
Tishri	1	First Day of New Year	Monday	Sept.	22
"	3	Fast of Gedaliah	Wednesday	"	24
"	10	Yom-Kippoor...................	Wednesday	Oct.	1
"	15	First Day of Tabernacle.........	Monday	"	6
"	21	Hoshannah-Rabbah.............	Sunday	"	12
"	22	Sh'mini-Atseres................	Monday	"	13
"	23	Simchas-Torah.................	Tuesday	"	14
Cheshvan.		Rosh-Chodesh....	Tues.-Wed.	"	21-22
Kislev.		Rosh-Chodesh	Thurs.-Fri.	Nov.	20-21
"	25	First Day of Chanukah..........	Monday	Dec.	15
Tebet.		Rosh-Chodesh	Sat.-Sun.	"	20-21
"	10	Fast of Tebet................·........	Tuesday	"	30
		1942.			
Sh'vat	1	Rosh-Chodesh	Monday	Jan.	19
Adar.		Rosh-Chodesh ......,.....	Tues.-Wed.	Feb.	17-18
"	13	Fast of Esther.............. ...	Monday	Mar.	2
"	14-15	Purim.........................	Tues.-Wed.	"	3-4
Nissan	1	Rosh-Chodesh	Thursday	"	19
"	15	First Day of Passover...........	Thursday	Apr.	2
Iyar.		Rosh-Chodesh	Fri.-Sat.	"	17-18
"	18	Lag-B'Omer................... 33d day of Omer.	Tuesday	May	5
Sivan	1	Rosh-Chodesh	Sunday	"	17
"	6	First Day of Pentecost..........	Friday·	"	22
Tammuz.		Rosh-Chodesh	Mon.-Tues.	June	15-16
"	17	Fast of Tammuz...............	Thursday	July	2
Av	1	Rosh-Chodesh....	Wednesday	"	15
"	9	Fast of Av....	Thursday	"	23
Ellul.		Rosh-Chodesh	Thurs.-Fri.	Aug.	13-14

EVENTFUL RECORDS.

CÆ. 43.—The people of Doris erected a statue of CLAUDIUS in the synagogue. PETRONIUS, the Roman governor of Syria, at the expostulation of AGRIPPA, ordered its removal and severely censured the inhabitants for the gross insult and offence offered to Judaism.

" 44.—AGRIPPA II. succeeded his father. CLAUDIUS endeavored to send him to Judea, but some court intrigues prevented him.

" 45.—AGRIPPA was sent to the government of Judea and Galilee. Judaism adopted by HELEN, Queen of Adiabena, and her son IZATES.

		1942.			
Tishri	1	First Day of New Year..........	Saturday	Sept.	12
"	3	Fast of Gedaliah................	Monday	"	14
"	10	Yom-Kippoor	Monday	"	21
"	15	First Day of Tabernacle	Saturday	"	26
"	21	Hoshannah-Rabbah	Friday	Oct.	2
"	22	Sh'mini-Atseres................	Saturday	"	3
"	23	Simchas-Torah	Sunday	"	4
Cheshvan.		Rosh-Chodesh	Sun.-Mon.	"	11-12
Kislev	1	Rosh-Chodesh	Tuesday	Nov.	10
"	25	First Day of Chanukah	Friday	Dec.	4
Tebet	1	Rosh-Chodesh	Wednesday	"	9
"	10	Fast of Tebet	Friday	"	18
		1943.			
Sh'vat	1	Rosh-Chodesh	Thursday	Jan.	7
Adar.		Rosh-Chodesh	Fri.-Sat.	Feb.	5-6
2d Adar.		Rosh-Chodesh	Sun. Mon.	Mar.	7-8
"	13	Fast of Esther................	Saturday*	"	20
"	14-15	Purim	Sun.-Mon.	"	21-22
Nissan	1	Rosh-Chodesh	Tuesday	Apr.	6
"	15	First Day of Passover...........	Tuesday	"	20
Iyar.		Rosh-Chodesh	Wed.-Thurs.	May	5-6
"	18	Lag-B'Omer...................	Sunday	"	23
		33d day of Omer.			
Sivan	1	Rosh-Chodesh	Friday	June	4
"	6	First Day of Pentecost..........	Wednesday	"	9
Tammuz.		Rosh-Chodesh	Sat.-Sun.	July	3-4
"	17	Fast of Tammuz	Tuesday	"	20
Av	1	Rosh-Chodesh	Monday	Aug.	2
"	9	Fast of Av	Tuesday	"	10
				"	31
Ellul.		Rosh-Chodesh	Tues.-Wed.	Sept.	1

* Observed Thursday previous.

EVENTFUL RECORDS.

C.Æ. 50.—A Roman soldier committed an indecency at the porch of the Temple, and the people in their indignation killed him; in consequence of which, a riot ensued with the Romans, and thirty thousand Jews were killed in Jerusalem.

" 55.—An order was issued at Rome for all Jews to leave the city. NERO confirmed the government of Galilee to AGRIPPA.

" 65.—Many Jews of rank were publicly whipped and 650 of them executed by order of FLORUS, the Roman governor of Judea. Owing to his bad government, the unfortunate wars took place with Rome which resulted in the final subjugation of the Jews by that great and powerful government.

5704 A.M.   1943-'44 CÆ.

			1943.			
Tishri	1	First Day of New Year	Thursday	Sept.	30
"	3	Fast of Gedaliah	Saturday*	Oct.	2
"	10	Yom-Kippoor	Saturday	"	9
"	15	First Day of Tabernacle	Thursday	"	14
"	21	Hoshannah-Rabbah	Wednesday	"	20
"	22	Sh'mini-Atseres	Thursday	"	21
"	23	Simchas-Torah	Friday	"	22
Cheshvan.		Rosh-Chodesh	Fri.-Sat.	"	29-30
Kislev	1	Rosh-Chodesh	Sunday	Nov.	28
"	25	First Day of Chanukah	Wednesday	Dec.	22
Tebet.		Rosh Chodesh	Mon.-Tues.	"	27-28
			1944.			
"	10	Fast of Tebet	Thursday	Jan.	6
Sh'vat	1	Rosh-Chodesh	Wednesday	"	26
Adar.		Rosh Chodesh	Thurs.-Fri.	Feb.	24-25
"	13	Fast of Esther	Wednesday	Mar.	9
"	14-15	Purim	Thurs.-Fri.	"	10-11
Nissan	1	Rosh-Chodesh	Saturday	"	25
"	15	First Day of Passover	Saturday	Apr.	8
Iyar.		Rosh-Chodesh	Sun.-Mon.	"	23-24
"	18	Lag-B'Omer	Thursday	May	11
		33d day of Omer.			
Sivan	1	Rosh-Chodesh	Tuesday	"	23
"	6	First Day of Pentecost	Sunday	"	28
Tammuz.		Rosh-Chodesh	Wed.-Thurs.	June	21-22
"	17	Fast of Tammuz	Saturday*	July	8
Av	1	Rosh-Chodesh	Friday	"	21
"	9	Fast of Av	Saturday*	"	29
Ellul.		Rosh-Chodesh	Sat.-Sun.	Aug.	19-20

* Observed following day.

EVENTFUL RECORDS.

CÆ. 65.—At Cæsarea alone twenty thousand were slaughtered; those who escaped death were made prisoners by FLORUS and sent to the galleys. At Scythopolis thirteen thousand were treacherously murdered in one night, and in other parts of Greece, large numbers were cruelly massacred. According to the " Mémoires de la Littérature," the Jews, about this time, first settled in China,* but M. DE GUIGNES supposes them to have done so 135 years before that. Father GAZONI states that at Cai-fong he met with a colony which is said to have been founded 206 years previous to the Christian era, also that he was shown an inscription dated 1515 cæ., in which the emperor assured

* "Mémoires de la Littérature," tome 48.

108

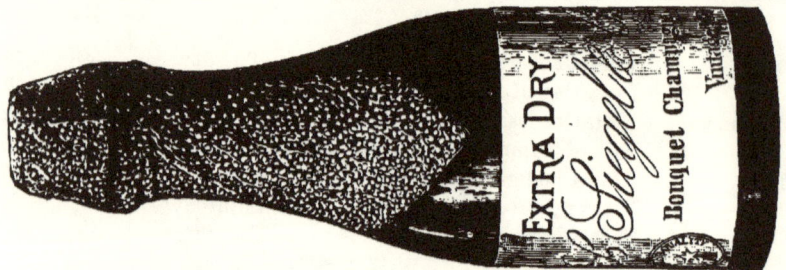

		1944.			
Tishri	1	First Day of New Year	Monday	Sept.	18
"	3	Fast of Gedaliah	Wednesday	"	20
"	10	Yom-Kippoor	Wednesday	"	27
"	15	First Day of Tabernacle	Monday	Oct.	2
"	21	Hoshannah-Rabbah	Sunday	"	8
"	22	Sh'mini-Atseres	Monday	"	9
"	23	Simchas-Torah	Tuesday	"	10
Cheshvan		Rosh-Chodesh	Tues.-Wed.	"	17-18
Kislev.		Rosh-Chodesh	Thurs.-Fri.	Nov.	16-17
"	25	First Day of Chanukah	Monday	Dec.	11
Tebet.		Rosh-Chodesh	Sat -Sun.	"	16-17
"	10	Fast of Tebet	Tuesday	"	26
		1945.			
Sh'vat	1	Rosh-Chodesh	Monday	Jan.	15
Adar.		Rosh-Chodesh	Tues -Wed.	Feb.	13-14
"	13	Fast of Esther	Monday	"	26
"	14-15	Purim	Tues.-Wed.	"	27-28
Nissan	1	Rosh-Chodesh	Thursday	Mar.	15
"	15	First Day of Passover	Thursday	"	29
Iyar.		Rosh-Chodesh	Fri.-Sat.	Apr.	13-14
"	18	Lag-B'Omer. 33d day of Omer.	Tuesday	May	1
Sivan	1	Rosh-Chodesh	Sunday	"	13
"	6	First Day of Pentecost	Friday	"	18
Tammuz.		Rosh-Chodesh	Mon.-Tues.	June	11-12
"	17	Fast of Tammuz	Thursday	"	28
Av	1	Rosh-Chodesh	Wednesday	July	11
"	9	Fast of Av	Thursday	"	19
Ellul.		Rosh-Chodesh	Thurs.-Fri.	Aug.	9-10

EVENTFUL RECORDS.

the Jews of his good-will and regard, complimenting them for their honor and fidelity in their various pursuits. their efficiency and upright conduct in many civil and military positions which they held, and also for their regular and faithful observance of their own religious duties.

C.Æ. 67.—The Roman forces in Judea were placed under' the command of VESPASIAN. JOTAPATA made a brave defence during 47 days of siege, 40,000 men being killed.

A fierce engagement took place on Lake Genesareth and 37,200 men were made captives. Of these 30,000 were sold as slaves, 6,000 were taken prisoners to Rome, and the remaining 1,200, being unfit for military service, were slain.

		1945.			
Tishri	1	First Day of New Year	Saturday	Sept.	8
"	3	Fast of Gedaliah..............	Monday	"	10
"	10	Yom-Kippoor	Monday	"	17
"	15	First Day of Tabernacle	Saturday	"	22
"	21	Hoshannah-Rabbah	Friday	"	28
"	22	Sh'mini-Atseres.............	Saturday	"	29
"	23	Simchas-Torah	Sunday	"	30
Cheshvan.		Rosh-Chodesh	Sun.-Mon.	Oct.	7-8
Kislev	1	Rosh-Chodesh	Tuesday	Nov.	6
"	25	First Day of Chanukah	Friday	"	30
Tebet	1	Rosh-Chodesh	Wednesday	Dec.	5
"	10	Fast of Tebet	Friday	"	14
		1946.			
Sh'vat	1	Rosh-Chodesh	Thursday	Jan.	3
Adar.		Rosh-Chodesh	Fri.-Sat.	Feb.	1-2
2d Adar.		Rosh-Chodesh....	Sun.-Mon.	Mar.	3-4
"	13	Fast of Esther..............	Saturday*	"	16
"	14-15	Purim	Sun.-Mon.	"	17 18
Nissan	1	Rosh-Chodesh	Tuesday	Apr.	2
"	15	First Day of Passover	Tuesday	"	16
Iyar.		Rosh-Chodesh	Wed.-Thurs.	May	1-2
"	18	Lag-B'Omer.............	Sunday	"	19
		33d day of Omer.			
Sivan	1	Rosh-Chodesh	Friday	"	31
"	6	First Day of Pentecost	Wednesday	June	5
Tammuz.		Rosh-Chodesh	Sat.-Sun.	"	29-30
"	17	Fast of Tammuz............ ...	Tuesday	July	16
Av	1	Rosh-Chodesh	Monday	"	29
"	9	Fast of Av	Tuesday	Aug.	6
Ellul.		Rosh-Chodesh	Tues.-Wed.	"	27-28

* Observed Thursday previous.

EVENTFUL RECORDS.

C.Æ. 68.—On the ninth day of *Av*, the fatal day on which the first Temple was destroyed 490 years previously, the second Temple was burned, 420 years after it was rebuilt. Jerusalem was conquered, the sacrifices ceased, and thousands of men, women, and children were mercilessly outraged and massacred. This, indeed, may be considered the most calamitous day in the Jewish calendar. Some writers place this in the year 70.

" 69.—MARIANA'S "Historia de España" states that many Jews, who had been sent captives into Spain, settled at Merida.

FRED. WENDEL,

PHOTOGRAPHER AND ARTIST,

841 BROADWAY,

Corner 13th Street,   NEW YORK.

Crayons, Pastels, and Copying Work a specialty.

SPECIAL TERMS TO PARTIES FORMING CLUBS OF 10 OR MORE.

C. F. TERHUNE.   G. H. WARNER.

WM. M. CRANE & CO.,

Gas Fixtures, Gas Stoves, Etc.,

BRASS GOODS, FENDERS, ANDIRONS,

GAS HEATERS, GAS LOGS, GAS RANGES,

838 BROADWAY,

Near 13th St.,   NEW YORK.

5707 A.M. 1946-'47 C.Æ.

		1946.			
Tishri	1	First Day of New Year	Thursday	Sept.	26
"	3	Fast of Gedaliah................	Saturday*	"	28
"	10	Yom-Kippoor....................	Saturday	Oct.	5
"	15	First Day of Tabernacle.........	Thursday	"	10
"	21	Hoshannah-Rabbah.............	Wednesday	"	16
"	22	Sh'mini-Atseres................	Thursday	"	17
"	23	Simchas-Torah.................	Friday	"	18
Cheshvan.		Rosh-Chodesh	Fri. Sat.	"	25-26
Kislev	1	Rosh-Chodesh	Sunday	Nov.	24
"	25	First Day of Chanukah	Wednesday	Dec.	18
Tebet.		Rosh-Chodesh	Mon.-Tues.	"	23-24
		1947.			
"	10	Fast of Tebet.................	Thursday	Jan.	2
Sh'vat	1	Rosh-Chodesh	Wednesday	"	22
Adar.		Rosh-Chodesh	Thurs.-Fri.	Feb.	20-21
"	13	Fast of Esther.................	Wednesday	Mar.	5
"	14-15	Purim.........................	Thurs.-Fri.	"	6-7
Nissan	1	Rosh-Chodesh	Saturday	"	22
"	15	First Day of Passover	Saturday	Apr.	5
Iyar.		Rosh-Chodesh	Sun.-Mon.	"	20-21
"	18	Lag-B'Omer .... 33d day of Omer.	Thursday	May	8
Sivan	1	Rosh-Chodesh	Tuesday	"	20
"	6	First Day of Pentecost..........	Sunday	"	25
Tammuz.		Rosh-Chodesh	Wed.-Thur.	June	18-19
"	17	Fast of Tammuz................	Saturday*	July	5
Av	1	Rosh-Chodesh	Friday	"	18
"	9	Fast of Av....................	Saturday*	"	26
Ellul.		Rosh-Chodesh	Sat.-Sun.	Aug.	16-17

* Observed day following.

EVENTFUL RECORDS.

C.Æ. , 71.—Preferring death to falling into the hands of the Romans, the male population of Masada first killed their wives and children and then themselves.

Judea was now finally subjugated, and it is calculated that in the various wars with the Romans the Jewish loss amounted to a million and a half. Of this number, only 100,000 were made captives, all the rest having sacrificed their lives in defence of their country and their faith, which is a striking proof of their patriotism and fidelity.

114

1947.

Tishri	1	First Day of New Year	Monday	Sept.	15
"	3	Fast of Gedaliah	Wednesday	"	17
"	10	Yom-Kippoor	Wednesday	"	24
"	15	First Day of Tabernacle	Monday	"	29
"	21	Hoshannah-Rabbah	Sunday	Oct.	5
"	22	Sh'mini-Atseres	Monday	"	6
"	23	Simchas Torah	Tuesday	"	7
Cheshvan.		Rosh-Chodesh	Tues.-Wed.	"	14-15
Kislev.		Rosh-Chodesh	Thurs.-Fri.	Nov.	13-14
"	25	First Day of Chanukah	Monday	Dec.	8
Tebet.		Rosh-Chodesh	Sat.-Sun.	"	13-14
"	10	Fast of Tebet	Tuesday	"	23

1948.

Sh'vat	1	Rosh-Chodesh	Monday	Jan.	12
Adar.		Rosh-Chodesh	Tues.-Wed.	Feb.	10-11
2d Adar.		Rosh-Chodesh	Thurs.-Fri.	Mar.	11-12
"	13	Fast of Esther .....,.........	Wednesday	"	24
"	14-15	Purim......	Thurs.-Fri.	"	25-26
Nissan	1	Rosh-Chodesh	Saturday	Apr.	10
"	15	First Day of Passover	Saturday	"	24
Iyar.		Rosh-Chodesh	Sun.-Mon.	May	9-10
"	18	Lag-B'Omer	Thursday	"	27
		33d day of Omer.			
Sivan	1	Rosh-Chodesh	Tuesday	June	8
"	6	First Day of Pentecost	Sunday	"	13
Tammuz.		Rosh-Chodesh	Wed.-Thurs	July	7-8
"	17	Fast of Tammuz	Saturday*	"	24
Av	1	Rosh-Chodesh	Friday	Aug.	6
"	9	Fast of Av....................	Saturday*	"	14
Ellul.		Rosh-Chodesh	Sat.-Sun.	Sept.	4-5

* Observed following day.

EVENTFUL RECORDS.

C.Æ.   71.—The census tax of half a shekel, which had been used for the purposes of the Holy Temple, was ordered by VESPASIAN to be taken towards the rebuilding of the Temple of JUPITER CAPITOLANUS, which had been destroyed about the same time.

"   100.—A son, or nephew, of the Emperor TITUS, named ONKELOS, was, at his own request, received as a convert to Judaism. He wrote the Chaldean paraphrase of the Pentateuch. His conversion is said to have taken place under the following

 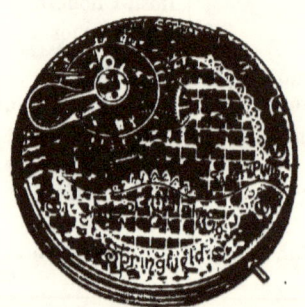

5709 A.M. 1948-'49 C.Æ.

		1948.			
Tishri	1	First Day of New Year	Monday	Oct.	
"	3	Fast of Gedaliah	Wednesday	"	
"	10	Yom-Kippoor	Wednesday	"	1
"	15	First Day of Tabernacle	Monday	"	1
"	21	Iloshannah-Rabbah	Sunday	"	2
"	22	Sh'mini-Atseres	Monday	"	2
"	23	Simchas-Torah	Tuesday·	"	2
Cheshvan.		Rosh-Chodesh....	Tues.-Wed.	Nov.	2-
Kislev.		Rosh-Chodesh	Thurs.-Fri.	Dec.	2-
"	25	First Day of Chanukah.	Monday	"	2
		1949:			
Tebet.		Rosh-Chodesh	Sat.-Sun.	Jan.	1-
"	10	Fast of Tebet..................	Tuesday	"	1
Sh'vat	1	Rosh-Chodesh	Monday	"	3
Adar.		Rosh-Chodesh ....,.....	Tues.-Wed.	Mar.	1-
"	13	Fast of Esther............. ...	Monday	"	1
"	14-15	Purim.........................	Tues.-Wed.	"	15-1
Nissan	1	Rosh-Chodesh	Thursday	"	3
··	15	First Day of Passover...........	Thursday	Apr.	1
Iyar.		Rosh-Chodesh	Fri.-Sat.	"	29 3
"	18	Lag-B'Omer.... .~........••.... 33d day of Omer.	Tuesday	May	1
Sivan	1	Rosh-Chodesh	Sunday	"	2
"	6	First Day of Pentecost..........	Friday	June	
Tammuz.		Rosh-Chodesh	Mon.-Tues.	"	27-2
"	17	Fast of Tammuz................	Thursday	July	1
Av	1	Rosh-Chodesh....	Wednesday	"	2
"	9	Fast of Av....	Thursday	Aug.	
Ellul.		Rosh-Chodesh	Thurs.-Fri.	"	25-2

EVENTFUL RECORDS.

circumstances. Having heard of the great fame of the cele
brated Rabbi HILLEL for extraordinary patience, he resolve
to put it to the test. Accordingly, just as the rabbi was pre
paring for the Sabbath eve, he went to him and expresse
his desire to embrace Judaism, provided he could be taugh
it in the short space of time that he could stand upon on
foot. This absurd request, he thought, would naturally ex
cite the rabbi's anger; but he was mistaken. HILLEL sim
ply answered him, " V'OHOVTO L'REYERCHO K'MOUCHO
(*Thou shalt love thy neighbor as thyself*), telling him thi

1949.

Tishri	1	First Day of New Year	Saturday	Sept.	24
"	3	Fast of Gedaliah	Monday	"	26
"	10	Yom-Kippoor	Monday	Oct.	3
"	15	First Day of Tabernacle	Saturday	"	8
"	21	Hoshannah-Rabbah	Friday	"	14
"	22	Sh'mini Atseres	Saturday	"	15
"	23	Simchas-Torah	Sunday	"	16
Cheshvan.		Rosh-Chodesh	Sun.-Mon.	"	23-24
Kislev	1	Rosh-Chodesh	Tuesday	Nov.	22
"	25	First Day of Chanukah	Friday	Dec.	16
Tebet	1	Rosh-Chodesh	Wednesday	"	21
"	10	Fast of Tebet	Friday	"	30

1950.

Sh'vat	1	Rosh-Chodesh	Thursday	Jan.	19
Adar.		Rosh-Chodesh	Fri.-Sat.	Feb.	17-18
"	13	Fast of Esther	Thursday	Mar.	2
"	14-15	Purim	Fri.-Sat.	"	3-4
Nissan	1	Rosh-Chodesh	Sunday	"	19
"	15	First Day of Passover	Sunday	April	2
Iyar.		Rosh-Chodesh	Mon.-Tues.	"	17-18
"	18	Lag-B'Omer	Friday	May	5
		33d day of Omer.			
Sivan	1	Rosh-Chodesh	Wednesday	"	17
"	6	First Day of Pentecost	Monday	"	22
Tammuz.		Rosh-Chodesh	Thurs.-Fri.	June	15-16
"	17	Fast of Tammuz	Sunday	July	2
Av	1	Rosh-Chodesh	Saturday	"	15
"	9	Fast of Av	Sunday	"	23
Ellul.		Rosh-Chodesh	Sun.-Mon.	Aug.	13-14

EVENTFUL RECORDS.

comprised Judaism, and that the practice of the forms and ceremonies connected with it were merely details, which he could study at leisure.

C.Æ. 115.—The Jews at Cyrene broke out in rebellion, which extended to Egypt, where they slew 220,000 Greeks. MARTIUS TURBO quelled the disturbance and restored order. They had killed, also, at Cyprus, 240,000 Greeks; but when HADRIAN regained possession of the island, he prohibited the Jews from relanding thereon under penalty of death.

5711 A.M. 1950-'51 C.Æ.

		1950.			
Tishri	1	First Day of New Year	Tuesday	Sept.	12
"	3	Fast of Gedaliah	Thursday	"	14
"	10	Yom-Kippoor	Thursday	"	21
"	15	First Day of Tabernacle	Tuesday	"	26
"	21	Hoshannah-Rabbah	Monday	Oct.	2
"	22	Sh'mini-Atseres	Tuesday	"	3
"	23	Simchas-Torah	Wednesday	"	4
Cheshvan.		Rosh-Chodesh	Wed-Thurs.	"	11-12
Kislev	1	Rosh-Chodesh	Friday	Nov.	10
"	25	First Day of Chanukah	Monday	Dec.	4
Tebet.		Rosh-Chodesh	Sat.-Sun.	"	9-10
"	10	Fast of Tebet	Tuesday	"	19
		1951.			
Sh'vat	1	Rosh-Chodesh	Monday	Jan.	8
Adar.		Rosh-Chodesh	Tues.-Wed.	Feb.	6-7
2d Adar.		Rosh-Chodesh	Thurs.-Fri.	Mar.	8-9
"	13	Fast of Esther	Wednesday	"	21
"	14-15	Purim	Thurs.-Fri.	"	22-23
Nissan	1	Rosh-Chodesh	Saturday	Apr.	7
"	15	First Day of Passover	Saturday	"	21
Iyar.		Rosh-Chodesh	Sun. Mon.	May	6-7
"	18	Lag-B'Omer	Thursday	"	24
Sivan	1	Rosh-Chodesh	Tuesday	June	5
"	6	First Day of Pentecost	Sunday	"	10
Tammuz.		Rosh-Chodesh	Wed.-Thurs.	July	4-5
"	17	Fast of Tammuz	Saturday*	"	21
Av	1	Rosh-Chodesh	Friday	Aug.	3
"	9	Fast of Av	Saturday*	"	11
Ellul.		Rosh-Chodesh	Sat.-Sun.	Sept.	1-2

33d day of Omer.

* Observed the following day.

EVENTFUL RECORDS.

C.Æ. 117.—Circumcision, the observance of the Sabbath, and the public reading of the Law were forbidden by HADRIAN on his becoming emperor. The punishment for permitting circumcision was to tie the children to their mothers' necks and throw them from the battlements, and the fathers were hanged. The reading of the Sabbatical portion of the Law being disallowed, the people substituted such portions of the prophets in place thereof, as were analogous to the section of the Law which would otherwise have been recited. These sections

1951.

Tishri	1	First Day of New Year	Monday	Oct.	1
"	3	Fast of Gedaliah	Wednesday	"	3
"	10	Yom-Kippoor	Wednesday	"	10
"	15	First Day of Tabernacle	Monday	"	15
"	21	Hoshannah-Rabbah	Sunday	"	21
"	22	Sh'mini-Atseres	Monday	"	22
"	23	Simchas-Torah	Tuesday	"	23
Cheshvan.		Rosh-Chodesh	Tues.-Wed.	"	30-31
Kislev.		Rosh-Chodesh	Thurs.-Fri.	Nov.	29-30
"	25	First Day of Chanukah	Monday	Dec.	24
Tebet.		Rosh-Chodesh	Sat.-Sun.	"	29-30

1952.

"	10	Fast of Tebet	Tuesday	Jan.	8
Sh'vat	1	Rosh-Chodesh	Monday	"	28
Adar.		Rosh-Chodesh	Tues.-Wed.	Feb.	26-27
"	13	Fast of Esther	Monday	Mar.	11
"	14-15	Purim	Tues.-Wed.	"	12-13
Nissan	1	Rosh-Chodesh	Thursday	"	27
"	15	First Day of Passover	Thursday	April	10
Iyar.		Rosh-Chodesh	Fri.-Sat.	"	25-26
"	18	Lag-B'Omer. 33d day of Omer.	Tuesday	May	13
Sivan	1	Rosh-Chodesh	Sunday	"	25
"	6	First Day of Pentecost	Friday	"	30
Tammuz.		Rosh-Chodesh	Mon. Tues.	June	23-24
"	17	Fast of Tammuz	Thursday	July	11
Av	1	Rosh-Chodesh	Wednesday	"	23
"	9	Fast of Av	Thursday	"	31
Ellul.		Rosh-Chodesh	Thurs.-Fri.	Aug.	21-22

EVENTFUL RECORDS.

were called the HAFTORAH, and when the public reading o
the weekly portion of the Law in the synagogue was resumed it was decided to continue reading the HAFTORAH
which custom still exists. From this custom probably arose
the Christian practice of reading in the church every Sunday
lessons from both the Old and New Testaments and portions
of the Epistles and Gospels.

C.Æ. 131.—The Messiahship was assumed by BAR-KOCHBA, who, finding
many adherents, held the Roman armies in Judea under sub-
jection for more than two years.

		1952.			
Tishri	1	First Day of New Year..........	Saturday	Sept.	20
"	3	Fast of Gedaliah................	Monday	"	22
"	10	Yom-Kippoor	Monday	"	29
"	15	First Day of Tabernacle	Saturday	Oct.	4
"	21	Hoshannah-Rabbah	Friday	"	10
"	22	Sh'mini-Atseres................	Saturday	"	11
"	23	Simchas-Torah	Sunday	"	12
Cheshvan.		Rosh-Chodesh	Sun.-Mon.	"	19-20
Kislev.		Rosh-Chodesh	Tues.-Wed.	Nov.	18-19
"	25	First Day of Chanukah	Saturday	Dec.	13
Tebet.		Rosh-Chodesh	Thurs.-Fri.	"	18-19
"	10	Fast of Tebet	Sunday	"	28
		1953.			
Sh'vat	1	Rosh-Chodesh	Saturday	Jan.	17
Adar.		Rosh-Chodesh	Sun. Mon.	Feb.	15-16
"	13	Fast of Esther................	Saturday*	"	28
"	14-15	Purim	Sun.-Mon.	Mar.	1-2
Nissan	1	Rosh-Chodesh	Tuesday	"	17
"	15	First Day of Passover..........	Tuesday	"	31
Iyar.		Rosh-Chodesh	Wed.-Thurs.	Apr.	15-16
"	18	Lag-B'Omer...................	Sunday	May	3
		33d day of Omer.			
Sivan	1	Rosh-Chodesh	Friday	"	15
"	6	First Day of Pentecost..........	Wednesday	"	20
Tammuz.		Rosh-Chodesh	Sat.-Sun.	June	13-14
"	17	Fast of Tammuz	Tuesday	"	30
Av	1	Rosh-Chodesh	Monday	July	13
"	9	Fast of Av	Tuesday	"	21
Ellul.		Rosh-Chodesh	Tues.-Wed.	Aug.	11-12

* Observed Thursday previous.

EVENTFUL RECORDS.

C.Æ. 134.—BAR-KOCHBAR took refuge at last in Bither, which was captured and destroyed on the fatal ninth of *Av*. This revolution, it is estimated, cost the lives of 600,000 Jews. The slaughter was terrible, and many days were occupied in burying the dead. Amongst the massacred were Rabbi AKIBA and nine others of note, who were subjected to the most horrible tortures previous to being slain.

The rebuilding of the city of Jerusalem ordered by HADRIAN.

B. FISCHER & CO.'S

BLACK PACKAGE

Russian Caravan Tea.

One Teaspoonful Makes THREE Cups.

HEALTHFULNESS.

83 Second Avenue.

MESSRS. B. FISCHER & Co,

GENTLEMEN: Your Russian Caravan Tea (Black Package) is without exception the finest and most wholesome Tea that has yet come to my notice; and I recommend it without hesitation.

Very Truly,

J. MOUNT BLEYER, M.D.

ECONOMY.

Hotel Marlborough, Broadway, 36th & 37th Sts.

Messrs. B. FISCHER & Co ,

GENTLEMEN: The great economy in the use of your Russian Caravan Tea combined with its delicious quality, makes it unequalled by any other Tea in this market for hotel use.

Very Truly Yours,

C. A. BLANCHARD & CO.

QUALITY.

"I find that the Black Package Russian Caravan Tea, imported by B. Fischer & Co , is the most delicious I have ever used."

LILLIAN RUSSELL.

SOLD BY ALL GOOD DEALERS.

		1953.			
Tishri	1	First Day of New Year	Thursday	Sept.	10
"	3	Fast of Gedaliah................	Saturday*	"	12
"	10	Yom-Kippoor...................	Saturday	"	19
"	15	First Day of Tabernacle.........	Thursday	"	24
"	21	Hoshannah-Rabbah..............	Wednesday	"	30
"	22	Sh'mini-Atseres.....	Thursday	Oct.	1
"	23	Simchas-Torah.................	Friday	"	2
Cheshvan.		Rosh-Chodesh	Fri.-Sat.	"	9-10
Kislev	1	Rosh-Chodesh	Sunday	Nov.	8
"	25	First Day of Chanukah..........	Wednesday	Dec.	2
Tebet	1	Rosh Chodesh	Monday	"	7
"	10	Fast of Tebet.	Wednesday	"	16
		1954.			
Sh'vat	1	Rosh-Chodesh	Tuesday	Jan.	5
Adar.		Rosh-Chodesh	Wed.-Thurs.	Feb.	3-4
2d Adar.		Rosh-Chodesh ....:..	Fri.-Sat.	Mar.	5-6
"	13	Fast of Esther	Thursday	"	18
"	14-15	Purim	Fri.-Sat.	"	19-20
Nissan	1	Rosh-Chodesh	Sunday	Apr.	4
"	15	First Day of Passover...........	Sunday	"	18
Iyar.		Rosh-Chodesh	Mon.-Tues.	May	3-4
"	18	Lag-B'Omer....................	Friday	"	21
		33d day of Omer.			
Sivan	1	Rosh-Chodesh	Wednesday	June	2
"	6	First Day of Pentecost.....,....·	Monday	"	7
Tammuz.		Rosh-Chodesh	Thurs.-Fri.	July	1-2
"	17	Fast of Tammuz	Sunday	"	18
Av	1	Rosh-Chodesh	Saturday	"	31
"	9	Fast of Av	Sunday	Aug.	8
Ellul.		Rosh-Chodesh	Thurs.-Fri.	"	29-30

* Observed following day.

EVENTFUL RECORDS.

C.E.   136.—He changed the name to ÆLIA CAPITOLANA, and on the site where the Holy Temple had stood he had one erected to JUPITER CAPITOLANUS. This caused a revolt of the Jews, who killed all the Romans in the city and destroyed the building. They were subdued by SEVERUS, upon which HADRIAN and the Roman Senate decreed that any Jew coming within sight of it should suffer death.

"   138.—ANTONINUS PIUS is said to have studied under Rabbi YEHUDAH HANASSI (Rabbi JUDAH, the Prince), and to have become a proselyte to Judaism. By his order the College of Jamni was opened, and all the ordinances of HADRIAN against the Jews were repealed.

		1954.			
Tishri	1	First Day of New Year	Tuesday	Sept.	28
"	3	Fast of Gedaliah	Thursday	"	30
"	10	Yom-Kippoor	Thursday	Oct.	7
"	15	First Day of Tabernacle	Tuesday	"	12
"	21	Hoshannah-Rabbah	Monday	"	18
"	22	Sh'mini-Atseres	Tuesday	"	19
"	23	Simchas-Torah	Wednesday	"	20
Cheshvan.		Rosh-Chodesh	Wed.-Thurs.	"	27-28
Kislev	1	Rosh-Chodesh	Friday	Nov.	26
"	25	First Day of Chanukah	Monday	Dec.	20
Tebet.		Rosh-Chodesh	Sat.-Sun.	"	25-26
		1955.			
"	10	Fast of Tebet	Tuesday	Jan.	4
Sh'vat	1	Rosh Chodesh	Monday	"	24
Adar.		Rosh-Chodesh	Tues.-Wed.	Feb.	22-23
"	13	Fast of Esther	Monday	Mar	7
"	14-15	Purim	Tues.-Wed.	"	8-9
Nissan	1	Rosh-Chodesh	Thursday	"	24
"	15	First Day of Passover	Thursday	Apr.	7
Iyar.		Rosh-Chodesh	Fri.-Sat.	"	22-23
"	18	Lag B'Omer. 33d day of Omer.	Tuesday	May	10
Sivan	1	Rosh-Chodesh	Sunday	"	22
"	6	First Day of Pentecost	Friday	"	27
Tammuz.		Rosh-Chodesh	Mon.-Tues.	June	20-21
"	17	Fast of Tammuz	Thursday	July	7
Av	1	Rosh-Chodesh	Wednesday	"	20
"	9	Fast of Av	Thursday	"	28
Ellul.		Rosh-Chodesh	Thurs. Fri.	Aug.	18-19

EVENTFUL RECORDS.

C.Æ. 141.*—Our great teacher, Rabbi YEHUDAH HANNASSI, compiled the MISHNA. His many virtues, sincere piety, and profound learning caused him to be much esteemed, especially by the Emperors ANTONINUS. AURELIUS, and COMMODUS.
Rabbi HILLEL founded the principles of the Jewish Almanac.

"19 6.—The enactments which ANTONINUS PIUS had issued in favor of the Jews were confirmed by SEVERUS. He also gave them all rights and privileges of Roman citizens, and held them exempt from all duties which such rights required of them when opposed to or interfering with their religious observances.

* Some claim 190 for this date.

5716 A.M. 1955-'56 C.Æ.

		1955.			
Tishri	1	First Day of New Year	Saturday	Sept.	17
"	3	Fast of Gedaliah	Monday	"	19
"	10	Yom-Kippoor....................	Monday	."	26
"	15	First Day of Tabernacle	Saturday	Oct.	1
"	21	Iloshannah-Rabbah..............	Friday	..	7
"	22	Sh'mini-Atseres. .,.............	Saturday	"	8
"	23	Simchas-Torah..................	Sunday.	"	9
Cheshvan.		Rosh-Chodesh	Sun.-Mon.	"	16 17
Kislev.		Rosh-Chodesh	Tues.-Wed.	Nov.	15-16
"	25	First Day of Chanukah	Saturday	Dec.	10
Tebet.		Rosh-Chodesh	Thurs.-Fri.	"	15-16
"	10	Fast of Tebet..................	Sunday	"	25
		1956.			
Sh'vat	1	Rosh-Chodesh	Saturday	Jan.	14
Adar.		Rosh-Chodesh	Sun.-Mon.	Feb.	12-13
"	13	Fast of Esther.................	Saturday*	"	25
"	14-15	Purim .,.....................	Sun.-Mon.	"	26-27
Nissan	1	Rosh-Chodesh	Tuesday	Mar.	13
"	15	First Day of Passover	Tuesday	"	27
Iyar.		Rosh-Chodesh ....,.......	Wed.-Thurs.	Apr.	11-12
..	18	Lag-B'Omer...................	Sunday	"	29
		33d day of Omer.			
Sivan	1	Rosh-Chodesh	Friday	May	11
"	6	First Day of Pentecost..........	Wednesday	"	16
Tammuz.		Rosh-Chodesh	Sat.-Sun.	June	9-10
"	17	Fast of Tammuz................	Tuesday	"	26
Av	1	Rosh-Chodesh	Monday	July	9
"	9	Fast of Av	Tuesday	"	17
Ellul.		Rosh-Chodesh	Tues.-Wed.	Aug.	7-8

* Observed Thursday previous.

EVENTFUL RECORDS.

C.Æ. 243.—Rabbi SAMUEL, at Nahardea, and Rabbi ADA, at Babylon, were notable as famous astronomers.

" 250.—The Jews were favored and protected by ZENOBIA, Queen of Palmyra, who is supposed to have been of Jewish descent.

" 277.—The Jews were forbidden by the Council of Elvira from offering their usual prayers for dew or rain.

" 297.—Judaism embraced by TOBBA, King of Yemen, in Arabia Felix, and introduced by him into his dominions.*

*"Mémoires de la Littérature," tom. 48.

132

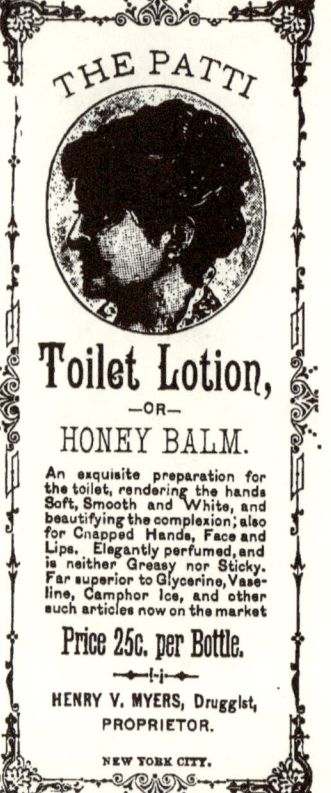

		1956.			
Tishri	1	First Day of New Year	Thursday	Sept.	6
``	3	Fast of Gedaliah...............	Saturday*	``	8
``	10	Yom-Kippoor..................	Saturday	``	15
``	15	First Day of Tabernacle.........	Thursday	``	20
``	21	Hoshannah-Rabbah.............	Wednesday	``	26
``	22	Sh'mini-Atseres...............	Thursday	``	27
``	23	Simchas-Torah.................	Friday	``	28
Cheshvan.		Rosh-Chodesh	Fri.-Sat.	Oct.	5-6
Kislev.		Rosh-Chodesh	Sun.-Mon.	Nov.	4-5
``	25	First Day of Chanukah.........	Thursday	``	29
Tebet.		Rosh-Chodesh..................	Tues.-Wed.	Dec.	4-5
``	10	Fast of Tebet.................	Friday	``	14
		1957.			
Sh'vat	1	Rosh-Chodesh	Thursday	Jan.	3
Adar.		Rosh-Chodesh	Fri.-Sat.	Feb.	1-2
2d Adar.		Rosh-Chodesh	Sun.-Mon.	Mar.	3-4
``	13	Fast of Esther................	Saturday*	``	16
``	14-15	Purim......	Sun.-Mon.	`` 17-18	
Nissan	1	Rosh-Chodesh	Tuesday	April	2
``	15	First Day of Passover...........	Tuesday	``	16
Iyar.		Rosh-Chodesh ....:...	Wed.-Thurs.	May	1-2
``	18	Lag-B'Omer .... 38d day of Omer.	Sunday	``	19
Sivan	1	Rosh-Chodesh	Friday	``	31
``	6	First Day of Pentecost..........	Wednesday	June	5
Tammuz.		Rosh-Chodesh	Sat.-Sun.	`` 29-30	
``	17	Fast of Tammuz	Tuesday	July	16
Av	1	Rosh-Chodesh	Monday	``	29
``	9	Fast of Av....................	Tuesday	Aug.	6
Ellul.		Rosh-Chodesh	Tues.-Wed.	`` 27-28	

* Observed following day.   † Observed Thursday previous.

EVENTFUL RECORDS.

C.Æ. 310.—The rebuilding of the Temple was commenced by CONSTANTINE.

`` 321.—Sunday, until then called the Lord's Day, was ordered to be observed as the Sabbath instead of Saturday. Both days had been previously kept by primitive Christians.

`` 322.—Rabbi JOSEPH, who, on account of his profound erudition, was named SINAI, existed at this time.

`` 325.—Easter day being observed by the Asiatic churches on the first day of the Jewish Passover, the Council of Nice ordered it thereafter to be observed on the first Sunday on or after the twenty-first day of March.

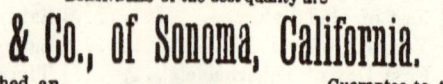

		1957.			
Tishri	1	First Day of New Year	Thursday	Sept.	26
"	3	Fast of Gedaliah................	Saturday*	"	28
"	10	Yom-Kippoor...................	Saturday	Oct.	5
"	15	First Day of Tabernacle..........	Thursday	"	10
"	21	Hoshannah-Rabbah..............	Wednesday	"	16
"	22	Sh'mini-Atseres................	Thursday	"	17
"	23	Simchas-Torah.................	Friday	"	18
Cheshvan.		Rosh-Chodesh	Fri.-Sat.	"	25-26
Kislev	1	Rosh-Chodesh	Sunday	Nov.	15
"	25	First Day of Chanukah	Wednesday	Dec.	9
Tebet.		Rosh-Chodesh	Mon.-Tues.	"	14-15
"	10	Fast of Tebet...................	Thursday	"	24
		1958.			
Sh'vat	1	Rosh-Chodesh	Wednesday	Jan.	13
Adar.		Rosh-Chodesh	Thurs.-Fri.	Feb.	11-12
"	13	Fast of Esther.................	Wednesday	"	24
"	14-15	Purim........................	Thurs.-Fri.	"	25-26
Nissan	1	Rosh-Chodesh	Saturday	Mar.	13
"	15	First Day of Passover	Saturday	"	27
Iyar.		Rosh-Chodesh	Sun.-Mon.	Apr.	11-12
"	18	Lag-B'Omer	Thursday	"	29
		33d day of Omer.			
Sivan	1	Rosh-Chodesh	Tuesday	May	11
"	6	First Day of Pentecost...........	Sunday	"	16
Tammuz.		Rosh Chodesh	Wed.-Thurs.	June	9-10
"	17	Fast of Tammuz................	Saturday*	"	26
Av	1	Rosh-Chodesh	Friday	July	9
"	9	Fast of Av....................	Saturday*	"	17
Ellul.		Rosh-Chodesh	Sat.-Sun.	Aug.	7-8

* Observed following day.

EVENTFUL RECORDS.

C.Æ. 353.—The edicts of HADRIAN against the Jews were renewed by CON-STANS, who also ordered that any Jew who married a Christian, or circumcised a slave, should be put to death.

" 355.—His oppression caused a revolt amongst the Jews of Diocæsarea. which was put down by GALLUS, who retook the city and burned it to the ground.

" 363.—Preparations to rebuild the Temple were commenced by JULIAN.

		1958.			
Tishri	1	First Day of New Year	Monday	Sept.	15
"	3	Fast of Gedaliah	Wednesday	"	17
"	10	Yom-Kippoor	Wednesday	"	24
"	15	First Day of Tabernacle	Monday	"	29
	21	Hoshannah-Rabbah	Sunday	Oct.	5
"	22	Sh'mini-Atseres	Monday	'	6
"	23	Simchas-Torah	Tuesday	"	7
Cheshvan.		Rosh-Chodesh	Tues.-Wed.	"	14-15
Kislev	1	Rosh-Chodesh	Thursday	Nov.	13
"	25	First Day of Chanukah	Sunday	Dec.	7
Tebet	1	Rosh-Chodesh	Friday	"	12
"	10	Fast of Tebet	Sunday	"	21
		1959.			
Sh'vat	1	Rosh-Chodesh	Saturday	Jan.	10
Adar.		Rosh-Chodesh	Sun.-Mon.	Feb.	8-9
2d Adar.		Rosh-Chodesh	Tues-Wed.	Mar.	10-11
"	13	Fast of Esther	Monday	"	23
"	14-15	Purim	Tues.-Wed.	"	24-25
Nissan	1	Rosh-Chodesh	Thursday	Apr.	9
"	15	First Day of Passover	Thursday	"	23
Iyar.		Rosh-Chodesh	Fri.-Sat.	May	8-9
"	18	Lag-B'Omer. 33d day of Omer.	Tuesday	"	26
Sivan	1	Rosh-Chodesh	Sunday	June	7
"	6	First Day of Pentecost	Friday	"	12
Tammuz.		Rosh-Chodesh	Thurs.-Fri.	July	6-7
"	17	Fast of Tammuz	Thursday	"	23
Av	1	Rosh-Chodesh	Wednesday	Aug.	5
"	9	Fast of Av	Thursday	"	13
Ellul.		Rosh-Chodesh	Thurs.-Fri.	Sept.	3-4

EVENTFUL RECORDS.

C.Æ. 365.—The former privileges of the Jews were accorded them by VALENTINIAN and VALENS, but they enforced the performance of public duties by the Jews when appointed to office.

" 379.—The Temple and the walls of Jerusalem were ordered by VALENTINIAN to be rebuilt.

" 388.—A synagogue at Rome having been wantonly burned, MAXIMUS ordered it to be rebuilt at the public expense.

The judicial court of the Jewish primate was empowered to punish members of its community, interference of the prefects being forbidden by THEODOSIUS THE GREAT.

[Continued from page 204.]

EVENTFUL RECORDS.

CÆ. 1189.—Jews were forbidden to enter Westminster Abbey at the coronation of RICHARD I. Some from the country places, supposing they might not be recognized, foolishly disobeyed the order, but were discovered and dragged out, and the people were so incensed that they maltreated every Jew they met, murdering many, plundering them, and then setting fire to their houses. The Lord Chief Justice and some nobles attempted to quell the riot by order of the king, but could not succeed for a considerable time. Three of the rioters were subsequently hanged.

" 1190.—Hearing that much wealth had been obtained by plundering the Jews in London, similar attacks were made upon them at Norwich, St. Edmondbury, Stamford, and Lincoln, in which latter place the governor protected them in the castle. At York the governor of the castle offered the same protection, and they accepted it. They discovered, however, that it was his intention to betray them, and they held possession of the fortress and refused him admission. They withstood a siege of several days, when, finding that they could no longer withstand it, they adopted the advice of their venerable rabbi, slew their wives, children, and themselves, having first burned all their valuables, then set the castle on fire to frustrate their persecutors and avoid their barbarities.

Don SOLOMON JACHIYA was appointed Generalissimo of the Portuguese forces.

" 1193.—At Bourges a Christian was executed by the authorities for the murder of a Jew, and in revenge for this act of justice PHILIP ordered eighty Jews to be burned.

" 1196.—The Duke of Austria appointed a Jew named SOLOMON as Major Domo.

" 1197.—At Norsa, in Italy, the Jewish population was plundered.

" 1198.—The Jews were invited by PHILIP AUGUSTUS to return to France.

" 1199.—In England the Chief Rabbi was appointed by royal commission, in which the king styled him "our friend and well beloved."[*]

Pope INNOCENT III. wrote to the Archbishop of Narbonne, forbidding compulsory baptism of the Jews, or their property being taken from them.

* "Anglia Judaica," p. 61.

1959.

Tishri	1	First Day of New Year	Saturday	Oct.	3
"	3	Fast of Gedaliah	Monday	"	5
"	10	Yom-Kippoor	Monday	"	12
"	15	First Day of Tabernacle	Saturday	"	17
"	21	Hoshannah-Rabbah	Friday	"	23
"	22	Sh'mini-Atseres	Saturday	"	24
"	23	Simchas-Torah	Sunday	"	25
Cheshvan.		Rosh-Chodesh	Sun.-Mon.	Nov.	1-2
Kislev.		Rosh-Chodesh	Tues.-Wed.	Dec.	1-2
"	25	First Day of Chanukah	Saturday	"	26
Tebet.		Rosh-Chodesh	Thurs.-Fri.	"	31
				{ 1960.	
				Jan.	1

1960.

"	10	Fast of Tebet	Sunday	"	10
Sh'vat	1	Rosh-Chodesh	Saturday	"	30
Adar.		Rosh-Chodesh	Sun.-Mon.	Feb.	28-29
"	13	Fast of Esther	Saturday*	Mar.	12
"	14-15	Purim	Sun.-Mon.	"	13-14
Nissan	1	Rosh-Chodesh	Tuesday	"	29
"	15	First Day of Passover	Tuesday	Apr.	12
Iyar.		Rosh-Chodesh	Wed.-Thurs.	"	27-28
"	18	Lag-B'Omer	Sunday	May	15
		33d day of Omer.			
Sivan	1	Rosh-Chodesh	Friday	"	27
"	6	First Day of Pentecost	Wednesday	June	1
Tammuz.		Rosh-Chodesh	Sat.-Sun.	"	25-26
"	17	Fast of Tammuz	Tuesday	July	12
Av	1	Rosh-Chodesh	Monday	"	25
"	9	Fast of Av	Tuesday	Aug.	2
Ellul.		Rosh-Chodesh	Tues.-Wed.	"	23-24

* Observed Thursday previous.

EVENTFUL RECORDS.

C.Æ. 395.—All rights and privileges given to the Jews by ARCADIUS and HONORIUS in their respective kingdoms. HONORIUS asserted that the glory of a prince consisted in permitting every society to enjoy quietly the privileges they had acquired, and that, although a religion might not be approved by a sovereign, he ought to preserve its privileges.

" 400.—Compilation of the TALMUD Yerushalmi begun.

" 408.—The populace pillaged a synagogue at Antioch.
Public demonstrations at Purim were forbidden by THEODOSIUS II.

CÆ. 1200.—The Jews paid 4,000 marks to King JOHN for a charter giving them the following rights : They were empowered thereby to hold land, to practise all their rites and customs, to go from place to place without interference or molestation, to be exempt from all tolls and taxes upon wines, and to have all their differences decided by their own rabbis, according to Jewish law.

" 1204.—King JOHN notified the Lord Mayor and barons of London that he would make them responsible for any injury to the Jews, who were being ill-treated there.

" 1205.—MOSES BEN MAIMON, the celebrated philosopher, died.

" 1210.—All Jews in England were ordered by JOHN to be imprisoned until they made a full disclosure of all their property; then, by most cruel tortures, he exacted from them 60,000 marks. At Bristol he forced 10,000 marks from one merchant by extracting one of his teeth daily, until he paid it.

" 1214.—FREDERICK II. of Germany extended his protection to the Jews.

" 1215.—In order to prevent illicit intercourse, the Jews were ordered by the Council of Lateran to wear a distinguishing badge.

" 1217.—At Toledo, Pope HONORIUS III. severely reprobated the massacre of the Jews.
The Turks took Jerusalem.
To protect the Jews from injury, and especially to guard them against insult from Jerusalem pilgrims, the sheriff, by order of HENRY III., appointed 24 burgesses in each city.

" 1218.—Another banishment of the Jews from France, but they were recalled by PHILIP II.

" 1220.—The noted commentator and grammarian, Rabbi DAVID KIMCHI, known as R'DAK, was held in high esteem at Narbonne for his great erudition. He translated the Bible into Spanish.
The bishop at Cologne fined the Jews of that city 4,200 pieces of silver upon an accusation that they had drowned a girl whose body was found in the Rhine.

" 1226.—Full liberty of conscience and numerous privileges were extended to the Jews by BOLESLAS, King of Lithuania, and the nobles likewise protected them from assaults.

" 1230.—The magnificent synagogue in London was converted into a church, and the Jews were compelled to contribute a third of their movable property into the exchequer.

1960.

Tishri	1	First Day of New Year	Thursday	Sept.	22
"	3	Fast of Gedaliah	Saturday*	"	24
"	10	Yom-Kippoor	Saturday	Oct.	1
"	15	First Day of Tabernacle	Thursday	"	6
"	21	Hoshannah-Rabbah	Wednesday	"	12
"	22	Sh'mini-Atseres	Thursday	"	13
"	23	Simchas-Torah	Friday	"	14
Cheshvan.		Rosh-Chodesh	Fri.-Sat.	"	21-22
Kislev.		Rosh-Chodesh	Sunday	Nov.	20
"	25	First Day of Chanukah.	Wednesday	Dec.	14
Tebet.		Rosh-Chodesh	Mon.-Tues.	"	19-20
"	10	Fast of Tebet..................	Thursday	"	29

1961.

Sh'vat.	1	Rosh-Chodesh	Wednesday	Jan.	18
Adar.		Rosh-Chodesh	Thurs.-Fri.	Feb.	16-17
"	13	Fast of Esther............... ...	Wednesday	Mar.	1
"	14-15	Purim.........................	Thurs.-Fri.	"	2-3
Nissan	1	Rosh-Chodesh	Saturday	"	18
"	15	First Day of Passover...........	Saturday	Apr.	1
Iyar.		Rosh-Chodesh	Sun.-Mon.	"	16-17
"	18	Lag-B'Omer...................	Thursday	May	4
		33d day of Omer.			
Sivan	1	Rosh-Chodesh	Tuesday	"	16
"	6	First Day of Pentecost...........	Sunday	"	21
Tammuz.		Rosh-Chodesh	Wed.-Thurs.	June	14-15
"	17	Fast of Tammuz...............	Saturday*	July	1
Av	1	Rosh-Chodesh....	Friday	"	14
"	9	Fast of Av....	Saturday*	"	22
Ellul.		Rosh-Chodesh	Sat.-Sun.	Aug.	11-12

* Observed following day

EVENTFUL RECORDS.

C.Æ. 412.—The building of new synagogues was forbidden by HONORIUS. He would not, however, permit those in use to be destroyed nor used for other purposes, nor would he allow the Jews to be compelled to violate their Sabbath.

" 415.—At Alexandria many Jews were murdered, and a large number, whose families had resided there since the time of ALEXANDER THE GREAT, were compelled to leave the city.

" 418.—The Jews, who were residing in large numbers at Port Mahon, were severely persecuted by SEVERUS, Bishop of Minorca, and their synagogue was destroyed.

C.Æ. 1232.—Eighteen thousand marks were extorted from the Jews by HENRY III.

" 1233.—JAMES I. of Aragon protected the Jews, and, it is said, used many of their prayers. He prohibited the Spanish version of the Bible.

" 1234.—One-third of all debts due to the Jews was confiscated by LOUIS IX.
They were prohibited from residing at Newcastle-on-Tyne.

" 1235.—At Norwich, England, the Jews were accused of crucifying a boy. The bishop hung four of them, and the populace destroyed their dwellings, although Parliament had acquitted them.

" 1236.—Pope GREGORY IX. said that Christians abused the name of religion to cover their avarice and enable them, under such pretext, to plunder the Jews, whom he declared innocent of the crimes charged against them. Many of them having been cruelly tortured and massacred in France, he wrote from Rieti to St. Louis : "The Christians exercise towards them the most unheard-of cruelties, forgetting that to the Jews they are indebted for the foundation of their own religion." He ordered the kings of Spain, France, and England to have all copies of the Talmud seized on the first Sunday of the following Lent.
Harming, plundering, or injuring Jews in any way, was prohibited by the Council of Tours.
The people of Southampton petitioned HENRY III. that Jews might not be allowed to reside there, and he granted their request.
NACHMANIDES, or Rabbi MOSES NACHMAN, styled RAMBAN, flourished at Genoa. He was the author of the noted commentary of the Pentateuch, called by his name, and several other valuable works.
At Fulda many Jews were murdered and burned.

" 1237.—HENRY III. again extorted from the Jews 10,000 marks.

" 1239.—All debts due to the Jews, by subjects of JOHN RUFUS of Brittany, were cancelled by him, and he ordered the judges not to inflict punishment on Christians for killing Jews. The year following he banished them.

" 1240.—Jews were prohibited demanding payment of debts due to them from the Crusaders, until their return, or authentic proof of their death.

1961.

Tishri	1	First Day of New Year	Monday	Sept.	11
"	3	Fast of Gedaliah................	Wednesday	"	13
"	10	Yom-Kippoor....................	Wednesday	" .	20
"	15	First Day of Tabernacle.........	Monday	"	25
"	21	Hoshannah-Rabbah.............	Sunday	Oct.	1
"	22	Sh'mini-Atseres.....	Monday	"	2
"	23	Simchas-Torah..................	Tuesday	"	3
Cheshvan.		Rosh-Chodesh	Tues.-Wed.	"	10-11
Kislev	1	Rosh-Chodesh	Thursday	Nov.	9
"	25	First Day of Chanukah.........	Sunday	Dec.	3
Tebet	1	Rosh Chodesh	Friday	"	8
"	10	Fast of Tebet.	Sunday	"	17

1962.

Sh'vat	1	Rosh-Chodesh	Saturday	Jan.	6
Adar.		Rosh-Chodesh	Sun.-Mon.	Feb.	4-5
2d Adar.		Rosh-Chodesh	Tues.-Wed.	Mar.	6-7
"	13	Fast of Esther	Monday	"	19
"	14-15	Purim	Tues.-Wed.	"	20-21
Nissan	1	Rosh-Chodesh	Thursday	Apr.	5
"	15	First Day of Passover...........	Thursday	"	19
Iyar.		Rosh-Chodesh	Fri.-Sat.	May	4-5
"	18	Lag-B'Omer...................	Tuesday	"	22
		33d day of Omer.			
Sivan	1	Rosh-Chodesh	Sunday	June	3
"	6	First Day of Pentecost.....	Friday	"	8
Tammuz.		Rosh-Chodesh	Mon.-Tues.	July	2-3
"	17	Fast of Tammuz	Thursday	"	19
Av	1	Rosh-Chodesh	Wednesday	Aug.	1
"	9	Fast of Av	Thursday	"	9
Ellul.		Rosh-Chodesh	Thurs.-Fri.	"	30-31

EVENTFUL RECORDS.

CÆ. 429.—Cessation of the Patriarchal power and authority.

" 469.—The TALMUD of Jerusalem completed.

> ST. HILAIRE, Bishop of Arles, had shown so much favor and given so much protection to the Jews that a special dirge or elegy was written by the Chief Rabbi at his death, and recited by the people at his grave.*

" 504.—The Babylonian Talmud, commonly called " *The Talmud*," was completed.

* Grégoire's " Cultes Religieuse," tom. 3.

EVENTFUL RECORDS.

C.E. 1241.—Six of the wealthiest Jews from all large cities and towns, and two from the smaller ones, were summoned by HENRY III. to meet at Worcester, on Sunday, February 10th. He addressed them as follows : "I want money. You must raise it, and have 10,000 marks ready for me at Midsummer and 10,000 marks at Michaelmas "

The houses of the Jews at Frankfort were set on fire, and nearly half the city was destroyed. One hundred and eighty Jews perished in the flames.

" 1245.—HENRY III. extorted 4,000 marks more.

" 1248.—At Paris, by order of Pope INNOCENT IV., twenty-four cart loads of the Talmud, then only in manuscript, were burned.

" 1250.—FREDERICK II. of Naples, on his death-bed, commended the Jews to the good will and protection of his son CONRAD, for great services which they had rendered him. CONRAD, deeming conversion to Christianity the greatest benefit he could bestow on them, ordered them to be baptized or quit his kingdom. He had the chief synagogue made into a church and dedicated it to STA. CATALINA.

" 1252.—A curious Chaldean work on the names, properties, and colors of 360 precious stones, was translated by JUDAH MOSEA, of Toledo. He was called the Hebrew CATO, and was physician to ALPHONSO X.

All Jews who were not mechanics were ordered to quit France.

The Jews of Germany were persecuted by CONRAD IV.

" 1255.—ISAAC BEN SAID, Chazan at Toledo, and others, composed the Alphonsine tables.

" 1256.—Translations into Latin of the astronomical works of AVICENA, and into Spanish of those of ACOSTA, on the celestial sphere, were made by Rabbi JUDAH COHEN, of Toledo.

" 1261.—In Languedoc and the southern provinces of France, Jews were declared eligible as magistrates.

" 1262.—In London the barons murdered 700 Jews and burned their chief synagogue in the Old Jewry.

" 1264.—The constable of the Tower of London gave an asylum to the Jews who were being plundered in that city, as well as at Northampton and Lincoln. The mayors of the different cities were ordered by HENRY to protect them from any outrage, and to issue a proclamation that "any who injured them should answer for it with life and limb."

		1962.			
Tishri	1	First Day of New Year..........	Saturday	Sept.	29
"	3	Fast of Gedaliah................	Monday	Oct.	1
"	10	Yom-Kippoor	Monday	"	8
"	15	First Day of Tabernacle	Saturday	"	13
"	21	Hoshannah-Rabbah	Friday	"	19
"	22	Sh'mini-Atseres................	Saturday	"	20
"	23	Simchas-Torah	Sunday	"	21
Cheshvan.		Rosh-Chodesh	Sun.-Mon.	"	28-29
Kislev.		Rosh-Chodesh	Tues.-Wed.	Nov.	27-28
"	25	First Day of Chanukah	Saturday	Dec.	22
Tebet.		Rosh-Chodesh	Thurs.-Fri.	"	27-28
		1963.			
"	10	Fast of Tebet	Sunday	Jan.	6
Sh'vat	1	Rosh-Chodesh	Saturday	"	26
Adar.		Rosh-Chodesh	Sun.-Mon.	Feb.	24-25
"	13	Fast of Esther.................	Saturday*	Mar.	9
"	14-15	Purim	Sun.-Mon.	"	10-11
Nissan	1	Rosh-Chodesh	Tuesday	"	26
"	15	First Day of Passover....	Tuesday	Apr.	9
Iyar.		Rosh-Chodesh ....,......	Wed.-Thurs.	"	24 25
"	18	Lag-B'Omer.............	Sunday	May	12
		33d day of Omer.			
Sivan	1	Rosh-Chodesh	Friday	"	24
"	6	First Day of Pentecost..........	Wednesday	"	29
Tammuz.		Rosh-Chodesh	Sat.-Sun.	June	22-23
"	17	Fast of Tammuz	Tuesday	July	9
Av	1	Rosh-Chodesh	Monday	"	22
"	9	Fast of Av	Tuesday	"	30
Ellul.		Rosh-Chodesh	Tues.-Wed.	Aug.	20-21

* Observed Thursday previous.

EVENTFUL RECORDS.

CÆ. 510.—By order of THEODORIC THE GREAT, a synagogue which had been burned at Rome was rebuilt, and others which had been robbed and pillaged at Milan and Genoa, were, by his direction, entirely renovated.

" 520.—An insurrection was caused among the Jews in Persia, by a pretender named MEIR claiming to be the Messiah. It was quelled by KOBAD, having lasted seven years.

" 535.—An edict was issued by JUSTINIAN to change all the synagogues in Africa into churches, and also that the Passover should be kept by the Jews on the same day that Easter was celebrated by the Christians.

C.E.   1264.—Jews were invited by JAMES I. of Aragon to settle in his kingdom.

The safety of the Jews in Poland was guaranteed them by a charter granted by BOLESLAS V.

"   1267.—The Council of Vienna issued an oppressive edict against the Jews.

"   1270.—Authority was given to the rabbis of England to issue *Cherem*, a ban of excommunication, against Jews who would not contribute towards the repairs of their public cemeteries.*

"   1275.—Rabbi ZAG, of Sujermenza, the mathematician, wrote on the astrolabium, water, and quicksilver clocks; and likewise translated several Arabian works on the science of astronomy.

"   1279.—EDWARD I. issued his barbarous edict.

On suspicion of clipping the coin of the realm, 280 Jews were executed in London.

"   1282.—Synagogues being held in many private residences, it was ordered by the archbishop of Canterbury that they should be suppressed, except one in each city. Upon this, the bishop of London destroyed all within his diocese, but was directed to allow one, which the Jews re-established.

"   1286.—The celebrated Rabbi MEIR (HOROM) flourished at Rottenburg.

Some Jews were murdered at Munich by an uprising of the people against them. The magistrates, finding themselves unable to quell the riot, advised them to retire to their synagogues, in which, notwithstanding the efforts of the duke to save them, they were all burned.

Rabbi JUDAH APENINI BADRASSI, of Bezeires, was so celebrated for his eloquence and oratory, that his Christian contemporaries titled him the Hebrew CICERO. He composed an epic poem on chess and was the author of some valuable works, among which is the *B'chenas Olom* (the Examination of the World).

"   1287.—The Jews throughout England were imprisoned.

"   1288.—EDWARD I. of England banished the Jews from Gascony.

At Paris they were fined for chanting too loudly in the synagogue.

* "Anglia Judaica," p. 127.

		1963.			
Tishri	1	First Day of New Year..........	Thursday	Sept.	19
"	3	Fast of Gedaliah	Saturday*	"	21
"	10	Yom-Kippoor	Saturday	"	28
"	15	First Day of Tabernacle.........	Thursday	Oct.	3
"	21	Hoshannah-Rabbah.............	Wednesday	"	9
"	22	Sh'mini Atseres	Thursday	"	10
"	23	Simchas-Torah.................	Friday	"	11
Cheshvan.		Rosh-Chodesh	Fri.-Sat.	"	18-19
Kislev	1	Rosh-Chodesh	Sunday	Nov.	17
"	25	First Day of Chanukah.........	Wednesday	Dec.	11
Tebet.		Rosh-Chodesh ....:	Mon.-Tues.	"	16-17
"	10	Fast of Tebet.................	Thursday	"	26
		1964.			
Sh'vat	1	Rosh-Chodesh	Wednesday	Jan.	15
Adar.		Rosh-Chodesh.................	Thurs.-Fri.	Feb.	13-14
"	13	Fast of Esther...............	Wednesday	"	26
"	14-15	Purim.......................	Thurs.-Fri.	"	27-28
Nissan	1	Rosh-Chodesh....	Saturday	Mar.	14
"	15	First Day of Passover..........	Saturday	"	28
Iyar.		Rosh-Chodesh...................	Sun.-Mon.	Apr.	12-13
"	18	Lag-B'Omer...................	Thursday	"	30
		33d day of Omer.			
Sivan	1	Rosh-Chodesh..	Tuesday	May	12
"	6	First Day of Pentecost..........	Sunday	"	17
Tammuz.		Rosh-Chodesh	Wed.-Thurs	June	10-11
"	17	Fast of Tammuz....	Saturday*	"	27
Av	1	Rosh-Chodesh....	Friday	July	10
"	9	Fast of Av....	Saturday*	"	18
Ellul.		Rosh-Chodesh.................	Sat.-Sun.	Aug.	8-9

*Observed following day.

EVENTFUL RECORDS.

C.Æ. 537.—BELISARIUS conquered Naples. The seaside defences had been courageously contested and held by the Jews, even when the other fortifications had surrendered. They were, however, eventually obliged to yield, and were mercilessly slaughtered, without distinction as to age or sex.

" 540.—In order to protect the Jews from the fanaticism of a mob in Paris, CHILDEBERT proclaimed that they should not leave their houses from Maundy Thursday until after Easter.

" 541.—For the same purpose, the Council at Orleans gave a similar order.

CÆ. 1288.—In Germany, on the accusation of having killed a Christian, the Jews were grossly ill-treated. The archbishop of Metz was ordered by the Emperor RUDOLPH to preach publicly that the accusation was false, and that they were not to be harmed.

The clergy were forbidden imposing fines on the Jews, by order of PHILIP IV. of France.

" 1290.—By order of EDWARD I., the Jews were banished from England, under pain of death; but he directed that they were to be treated honestly and kindly, and not to be overcharged for their passage or freight; also that the poor were to be conveyed at rates according to their means. It is estimated that about 16,000 departed in one day, October 9th.

" 1291.—By force of arms, the city of Berne was compelled by the Emperor ADOLPHUS to readmit the Jews whom it had exiled.

" 1292.—During a war between ADOLPHUS of Nassau and ALBERT of Austria, a peasant named FLEISCH incited the people of Franconia against the Jews. Several had their houses set on fire, whole families perished in the flames, and half of the city of Nuremberg was destroyed by the conflagration. The cities of Nieumark, Rottenburg, and Amberg were heavily fined by the duke after tranquillity had been restored.

" 1304.—Rabbi SOLOMON BEN ADERETH, celebrated for his erudition, and known as RASHBA, flourished at Barcelona.

Rabbi ASHER, of Rottenburg, titled RABINA ASHER, left Germany to settle in Spain, and, in consequence of his profound knowledge and deep learning, was appointed chief of the college at Toledo.

" 1306.—All property of Jews in France was seized by PHILIP IV., who banished them, only permitting them to take their clothing and sufficient means to carry them out of his kingdom. Their synagogues at Paris were converted into churches and their cemeteries desecrated. He recalled them during the following year.

" 1309.—Through the intercession of ROBERT, King of Naples and Jerusalem, the edict of banishment from the Papal States was rescinded, upon the payment by them of 10,000 crowns.

The Jews were granted many privileges, and the town of Gemappe was given them to reside in by JOHN II of Brabant, who afterwards went to their assistance and defeated the Knights of the Cross, who had attacked them.

The celebrated mathematician and astronomer, Rabbi ISAAC ISRAELI, flourished at Toledo.

		1964.			
Tishri	1	First Day of New Year..........	Monday	Sept.	7
"	3	Fast of Gedaliah	Wednesday	"	9
"	10	Yom-Kippoor	Wednesday	"	16
"	15	First Day of Tabernacle	Monday	"	21
"	21	Hoshaunah-Rabbah	Sunday	"	27
"	22	Sh'mini-Atseres.................	Monday	"	28
"	23	Simchas-Torah...................	Tuesday	"	29
Cheshvan.		Rosh-Chodesh	Tues.-Wed.	Oct.	6-7
Kislev.		Rosh-Chodesh	Thurs.-Fri.	Nov.	5-6
"	25	First Day of Chanukah	Monday	"	30
Tebet.		Rosh-Chodesh	Sat.-Sun.	Dec.	5-6
"	10	Fast of Tebet..................	Tuesday	"	15
		1965.			
Sh'vat	1	Rosh-Chodesh	Monday	Jan.	4
Adar.		Rosh-Chodesh	Tues.-Wed.	Feb.	2-3
2d Adar.		Rosh-Chodesh	Thurs. Fri.	Mar.	4-5
"	13	Fast of Esther.................	Wednesday	"	17
"	14-15	Purim	Thurs.-Fri.	"	18-19
Nissan	1	Rosh-Chodesh	Saturday	Apr.	3
"	15	First Day of Passover...........	Saturday	"	17
Iyar.		Rosh-Chodesh	Sun.-Mon.	May	2-3
"	18	Lag-B'Omer...................	Thursday	"	20
		33d day of Omer.			
Sivan	1	Rosh-Chodesh................	Tuesday	June	1
"	6	First Day of Pentecost.	Sunday	"	6
				"	30
Tammuz.		Rosh-Chodesh	Wed.-Thurs.	July	1
"	17	Fast of Tammuz................	Saturday*	"	17
Av	1	Rosh-Chodesh	Friday	"	30
"	9	Fast of Av	Saturday*	Aug.	7
Ellul.		Rosh-Chodesh	Sat.-Sun.	"	28 29

* Observed following day.

EVENTFUL RECORDS.

C.Æ.   555.—At Cæsarea the churches were destroyed and the governor and many of the inhabitants killed by the Jews, who had revolted. A great many were killed and a large number banished, and their property confiscated by ADAMANTIUS, who had been commissioned against them.

"   580.—Jews settled about this time at Cochin and on the coast of Malabar.

"   582.—Those who refused to embrace Christianity were greatly persecuted by CHILPERIC.

CÆ. 1311.—Jews again banished from France.

" 1314.—LOUIS X. invited them to return.

" 1320.—A body of fanatics, called the Shepherds, cruelly massacred many Jews and put others to torture. At Verdun, a tragedy was enacted similar to the one at York in 1190, but on their approach to Avignon, Pope JOHN XXII. put a stop to the barbarities by his anathemas.

By order of Pope JOHN XXII., manuscripts of the Talmud in Italy were burned.

" 1321.—At Provence, Languedoc, and Aquitaine many Jews were burned and murdered upon a charge of having poisoned the rivers.

" 1322.—Rabbi LEVI BEN GERSHON, a celebrated commentator, surnamed RALBAG, flourished at Perpignan.

At Paris the Jews were imprisoned and compelled by PHILIP V. to prove all debts due to them, which he then seized. He secured thereby 150,000 francs, and then condemned many of the victims to the flames.

" 1333.—ALPHONSO II. appointed a Jew, JOSEPH DE ASTIGI, Intendant of Finance.

" 1339.—Persecution of the Jews, forbidden by the bishop of Spires.

" 1340.—Rabbi DAVID ABUDARHAM, author of a learned work on our ritual, and a noted astronomer, was celebrated at Seville.

Rabbi BECHAYAI, son of Rabbi ASHER and known as RABINU BECHAYAI HADAYAN, at Barcelona, was chief of all Jews in Spain.

" 1344.—Jews banished by LOUIS I. of Hungary.

" 1348.—An accusation was made against the Jews in France of causing plague by poisoning the rivers. Many were cruelly slaughtered and the rest of them banished on July 22d. They were received kindly at Avignon by Pope CLEMENT VI., who severely condemned the atrocities which had been committed, and he was called by them their father and comforter.

" 1349.—In order to avoid the barbarities of the populace, which ALPHONSO was unable to restrain, the family of Rabbi ASHER destroyed themselves at Toledo. At Spires, Strassburg, and Frankfort, the Jews were plundered and burned by the Flagellants, and many were massacred at Brabant and Franconia. At Frankfort many public edifices were destroyed by the conflagration.

		1965.			
Tishri	1	First Day of New Year..........	Monday	Sept.	27
"	3	Fast of Gedaliah	Wednesday	"	29
"	10	Yom-Kippoor...................	Wednesday	Oct.	6
"	15	First Day of Tabernacle.........	Monday	"	11
"	21	Hoshannah-Rabbah.............	Sunday	"	17
"	22	Sh'mini-Atseres................	Monday	"	18
"	23	Simchas-Torah.................	Tuesday	"	19
Cheshvan.		Rosh-Chodesh	Tues.-Wed.	"	26-27
Kislev	1	Rosh-Chodesh	Thursday	Nov.	25
"	25	First Day of Chanukah	Sunday	Dec.	19
Tebet	1	Rosh-Chodesh	Friday	"	24
		1966.			
"	10	Fast of Tebet.................	Sunday	Jan.	2
Sh'vat	1	Rosh-Chodesh	Saturday	"	22
Adar.		Rosh-Chodesh	Sun.-Mon.	Feb.	20-21
"	13	Fast of Esther................	Saturday*	Mar.	5
"	14-15	Purim	Sun.-Mon.	"	6-7
Nissan	1	Rosh-Chodesh	Tuesday	"	22
"	15	First Day of Passover	Tuesday	Apr.	5
Iyar.		Rosh-Chodesh	Wed.-Thurs.	"	28-29
"	18	Lag-B'Omer...................	Sunday	May	8
		33d day of Omer.			
Sivan	1	Rosh-Chodesh	Friday	"	20
"	6	First Day of Pentecost..........	Wednesday	"	25
Tammuz.		Rosh-Chodesh	Sat.-Sun.	June	18-19
"	17	Fast of Tammuz................	Tuesday	July	5
Av	1	Rosh-Chodesh	Monday	"	18
"	9	Fast of Av	Tuesday	"	26
Ellul.		Rosh-Chodesh ....,....	Tues.-Wed.	Aug.	16-17

* Observed Thursday previous.

EVENTFUL RECORDS.

C.Æ. 589.—Jews were much oppressed and their schools of learning closed by CHOSROES THE GREAT.

" 590.—They found great favor and received much kindness from HOMIDAS III., who reopened their academies.

" 591.—A renegade Jew was baptized at Cagliari, and placed images of MARY and some saints in the synagogue the following day. The act of desecration was brought under the notice of Pope GREGORY THE GREAT, who directed the bishops to cause their removal, and he further ordered that all synagogues then in existence should be protected, the law, at that time, forbidding the erection of new ones.

C.Æ. 1351.—A treaty was made by JOHN II. with the Jews, to readmit them into France and permit them to enjoy all the former privileges, upon payment of fourteen florins for a man and wife, one florin each for children and servants, and an annual payment of seven florins. They were permitted to hold landed property and were free of all taxes, except on land.

" 1356.—The Jews were recalled by JOHN of Normandy, but he soon again banished them.

" 1364.—The treaty made by JOHN II., renewed by CHARLES V. of France, first for six and afterwards for ten years.

Many privileges were granted the Jews by CASIMIR III. of Poland, who obtained protection for them from Pope URBAN V. against the attacks of the clergy. He took a Jewess named ESTHER for a mistress.

" 1369.—The Jews who defended Burgos for PETER THE CRUEL, would not surrender it to HENRY of Trastemar, his natural brother, until assured of the death of their legitimate sovereign. This loyalty on their part caused HENRY to afford them his protection.

. " 1379.—His physician, DON MEIR, being suspected or charged with poisoning him, his brother, JOHN I., who succeeded him, was about to banish the Jews, which they avoided by the payment of 50,000 crowns.

" 1389.—At Prague, on the first day of Passover, a synagogue was burned whilst full of people. The cemeteries were desecrated, and many slew their families and destroyed themselves, in order to avoid their barbarous persecutors. At Ulm every one was burned in their houses, and 12,000 were murdered at Metz.

" 1391.—All debts, due from the nobility to the Jews, were cancelled by WINCELAUS.

At Spires, excepting some children who were baptized, all were slaughtered, and many were massacred at Gotha, in Saxony.

In many parts of Spain, owing to the persecution of HENRY III. of Castile, many Jews were murdered. Numbers who escaped settled in Algiers and were governed there by their own judges.

" 1392.—At Seville and Cordova, the civil power was unable to restrain the populace from plunder and murder of the Jewish in- habitants.

" 1394.—Jews banished from France by order of CHARLES VI.

The archdeacon of Ecija was arrested and punished for inciting the populace against them.

		1966.			
Tishri	1	First Day of New Year	Thursday	Sept.	15
"	3	Fast of Gedaliah...............	Saturday*	"	17
"	10	Yom-Kippoor..................	Saturday	"	24
"	15	First Day of Tabernacle.........	Thursday	"	29
"	21	Hoshannah-Rabbah..............	Wednesday	Oct.	5
"	22	Sh'mini-Atseres.............	Thursday	"	6
"	23	Simchas Torah.................	Friday	"	7
Cheshvan.		Rosh-Chodesh	Fri.-Sat.	"	14-15
Kislev.		Rosh-Chodesh	Sun.-Mon.	Nov.	13-14
"	25	First Day of Chanukah.........	Thursday	Dec.	8
Tebet.		Rosh-Chodesh...................	Tues.-Wed.	"	13-14
"	10	Fast of Tebet..................	Friday	"	23
		1967.			
Sh'vat	1	Rosh-Chodesh	Thursday	Jan.	12
Adar.		Rosh-Chodesh	Fri.-Sat.	Feb.	10-11
2d Adar.		Rosh-Chodesh	Sun.-Mon.	Mar.	12-13
"	13	Fast of Esther.................	Saturday†	"	25
"	14-15	Purim......	Sun.-Mon.	"	26-27
Nissan	1	Rosh-Chodesh	Tuesday	Apr.	11
"	15	First Day of Passover...........	Tuesday	"	25
Iyar.		Rosh-Chodesh	Wed.-Thurs.	May	10-11
"	18	Lag-B'Omer .... 33d day of Omer.	Sunday	"	28
Sivan	1	Rosh-Chodesh	Friday	June	9
"	6	First Day of Pentecost..........	Wednesday	"	14
Tammuz.		Rosh-Chodesh	Sat.-Sun.	July	8-9
"	17	Fast of Tammuz	Tuesday	"	25
Av	1	Rosh-Chodesh	Monday	Aug.	7
"	9	Fast of Av....................	Tuesday	"	15
Ellul.		Rosh-Chodesh	Tues.-Wed.	Sept.	5-6

* Observed following day.   † Observed Thursday previous.

EVENTFUL RECORDS.

C.Æ. 603.—The Jews of various places were invited by WITTIZA to settle in Spain.

" 611.—Jerusalem was taken and the churches destroyed by CHOSROES II., who received assistance from the Jews.

" 615.—Many Jews were cruelly tortured by MAHODES on his taking New Antioch; others were slain, and the remainder were sold as slaves.

" 618.—The Jews of Spain who refused to be Christianized were compelled by SIZEBUT, the king, to quit the country. Many whose families had been settled in France and Africa for nearly six hundred years, went there.

C.Æ. 1394.—At Bologna, where for many years the Jews had been highly favored and protected, they built a magnificent synagogue.

The king of Fez established at Mequinez a superior court for governing the Jews, under the superintendence of their Chief Rabbi.

" 1400.—Permission to establish a bank was granted to the Jews at Venice.

The Emperor ROBERT banished them from the German Empire.

" 1405.—The *Ethics* of ARISTOTLE were translated into Hebrew by Rabbi MEIR ALVARES, physician to HENRY III. of Castile.

" 1410.—LADISLAS permitted the Jews to settle in Naples.

" 1415.—The Anti-Pope, BENEDICT XIII., published his inhuman bull.

At Saragossa, Rabbi JOSEPH ALBO flourished. He was the author of a learned work on the *Sifar Ikarim* (Articles of Faith).

Thirty thousand Jews are said to have been baptized in order to save their lives from the fury of the populace, who were instigated against them by Friar VINCENT FERRER.

" 1416.—The Queen Regent of Spain employed many Jews at court, which aroused the jealousy of the nobility, who caused their persecution at Segovia.

" 1417.—A book of the Law was presented by the Grand Rabbi to Pope MARTIN V. on his installation, from which circumstance many popes afterwards demanded the same honor. In receiving the gift, the Pope replied: "I honor and reverence the Law you received from God, but condemn your exposition of it."

" 1420.—Murder of many Jews and banishment of the rest from Alexandria.

" 1430.—At Aix, in Provence, they were plundered and many forcibly baptized.

" 1434.—All connection between Jews and Christians was prohibited by the Council of Basle.

" 1448.—Jews were protected by Pope NICHOLAS V. in all States. He also wrote to Spain that "they should not be forced to abjure their religion, and that they had the right to be admitted to public offices."

" 1450.—In Spain and Portugal the Jews who were baptized were called New Christians.

An act was passed at Toledo that no public office could be filled by a Jew, and many of them there were massacred.

" 1451.—Jews banished from Silesia, after many had been plundered and murdered.

		1967.			
Tishri	1	First Day of New Year	Thursday	Oct.	5
"	3	Fast of Gedaliah................	Saturday*	"	7
"	10	Yom-Kippoor....................	Saturday	"	14
"	15	First Day of Tabernacle..........	Thursday	"	19
"	21	Hoshannah-Rabbah..............	Wednesday	"	25
"	22	Sh'mini-Atseres.................	Thursday	"	26
"	23	Simchas-Torah..................	Friday	"	27
Cheshvan.		Rosh-Chodesh	Fri.-Sat.	Nov.	3-4
Kislev	1	Rosh-Chodesh	Sunday	Dec.	3
"	25	First Day of Chanukah	Wednesday	"	27
		1968.			
Tebet.		Rosh-Chodesh	Mon.-Tues.	Jan.	1-2
"	10	Fast of Tebet..................	Thursday	"	11
Sh'vat	1	Rosh-Chodesh	Wednesday	"	31
Adar.		Rosh-Chodesh	Thurs.-Fri.	{ Feb. / Mar.	29 / 1
"	13	Fast of Esther..................	Wednesday	"	13
"	14-15	Purim.............................	Thurs.-Fri.	"	14-15
Nissan	1	Rosh-Chodesh	Saturday	"	30
"	15	First Day of Passover	Saturday	Apr.	13
Iyar.		Rosh-Chodesh	Sun.-Mon.	"	28-29
"	18	Lag-B'Omer........ .... 33d day of Omer.	Thursday	May	16
Sivan	1	Rosh-Chodesh	Tuesday	"	28
"	6	First Day of Pentecost............	Sunday	June	2
Tammuz.		Rosh-Chodesh	Wed.-Thurs.	"	26-27
"	17	Fast of Tammuz................	Saturday*	July	13
Av	1	Rosh-Chodesh	Friday	"	26
"	9	Fast of Av.....................	Saturday*	Aug.	3
Ellul.		Rosh-Chodesh	Sat.-Sun.	"	24-25

* Observed following day.

EVENTFUL RECORDS.

C.Æ.   622.—The Mohammedan era commenced, and there was a persecution of the Jews to compel them to embrace Mohammedanism.

"   627.—The decree of HADRIAN, prohibiting the Jews approaching within a league of Jerusalem, was enforced by HERACLIUS on his taking the city.

"   631.—It having been predicted by an astrologer that Christendom would be destroyed by a nation which had been circumcised, the Jews were, in consequence, persecuted by HERACLIUS.

C.Æ. 1454.—Jews ordered by Lewis X. to quit forty cities of Bavaria at one hour of the same day.

" 1472.—At Venice they received protection from the Doge and Senate, who ordered the authorities of Padua to treat them the same as all other subjects.

The Jews having gallantly defended Buda, in behalf of the Turks, from the attacks of the Christians, they were, in revenge, banished from Trent by the latter at three hours' notice.

Bajazet II. selected a Jew as his physician.

The author of the *Menoros Hamour* (the Lamp of Light), R. Isaac Aboab, flourished at Castile.

" 1479.—Ferdinand of Aragon was successfully operated on for cataract by Dr. Abiatar, a Jewish physician of Merida.

" 1480.—Establishment of the Spanish Inquisition at Seville. Those condemned by it were burned, it being forbidden by the Scriptures to shed human blood.

" 1482.—At Castile, Abraham Senior was appointed receiver-general of the revenue.

" 1484.—Rabbi Don Isaac Abarbanel was appointed finance minister to Ferdinand and Isabella. He had fled from Portugal two years previously to avoid the fate which the other ministers of Alphonso V. suffered from John II.

" 1485.—The celebrated historian, astronomer, and physician, Rabbi Solomon ben Virga, flourished in Spain.

" 1486.—The first book printed in Hebrew, at Soncino, near Cremona.

" 1488.—On taking Malaga from the Moors, the New Christians who had gone there and returned to Judaism, were burned by the Inquisition.

" 1491.—The great mathematician, astronomer, and physician, Bonnet de Lates, the inventor of the astronomical ring, flourished.

The New Christians fled for protection to the dominions of the Duke of Medina Sidonia, and made a treaty for the purchase of the town and fortress of Gibraltar. When it was ready for signature the populace compelled the duke to break it off.

" 1492.—The following edict of Ferdinand and Isabella was the most severe calamity which befell the Jews since their dispersion: "Seeing that the Jews of our States induce many Christians, especially the nobles of Andalusia, to embrace Judaism, for this they are banished under the severest penalties."

		1968.			
Tishri	1	First Day of New Year	Monday	Sept.	23
"	3	Fast of Gedaliah................	Wednesday	"	25
"	10	Yom-Kippoor	Wednesday	Oct.	2
"	15	First Day of Tabernacle	Monday	"	7
"	21	Hoshannah-Rabbah	Sunday	"	13
"	22	Sh'mini-Atseres..........	Monday	"	14
"	23	Simchas-Torah	Tuesday	"	15
Cheshvan.		Rosh-Chodesh	Tues.-Wed.	"	22-23
Kislev.		Rosh-Chodesh	Thurs.-Fri.	Nov.	21-22
"	25	First Day of Chanukah	Monday	Dec.	16
Tebet.		Rosh-Chodesh	Sat.-Sun.	"	21-22
"	10	Fast of Tebet	Tuesday	"	31
		1969.			
Sh'vat	1	Rosh-Chodesh	Monday	Jan.	20
Adar.		Rosh-Chodesh	Tues -Wed.	Feb.	18-19
"	13	Fast of Esther.................	Monday	Mar.	3
"	14-15	Purim	Tues.-Wed.	"	4-5
Nissan	1	Rosh-Chodesh	Thursday	"	20
"	15	First Day of Passover	Thursday	Apr.	3
Iyar.		Rosh-Chodesh	Fri.-Sat.	"	18-19
"	18	Lag-B'Omer	Tuesday	May	6
		33d day of Omer.			
Sivan		Rosh-Chodesh	Sunday	"	18
"	6	First Day of Pentecost	Friday	"	23
Tammuz.		Rosh-Chodesh	Mon.-Tues.	June	16-17
"	17	Fast of Tammuz.......... ...	Thursday	July	3
Av	1	Rosh-Chodesh	Wednesday	"	16
"	9	Fast of Av	Thursday	"	24
Ellul.		Rosh-Chodesh	Thurs.-Fri.	Aug.	14-15

EVENTFUL RECORDS.

C.Æ. 633.—An order was made by the Council of Toledo by which the Jews were freed from being baptized, but they were not allowed to hold any public office.

The Jews were compelled to become Christians or quit France. This was the act of DAGOBERT, instigated by HERACLIUS.

" 636.—The Council of Toledo administered an oath to the king, on his accession, that he would not favor the Jews, and that none except those who professed Christianity should be allowed any freedom in his dominions.

" 652.—A Jew purchased from the Saracens, the Colossus of Rhodes.

CÆ. 1492. The penalty was death, if found in the kingdom of Spain after four months, unless they embraced Christianity. Christians were prohibited by the Inquisitor TORQUEMADA from supplying them after the month of April with bread, water, meat, or wine. When all appeals for justice and humanity failed to have any effect upon the royal pair, ABARBANEL, by an offer of 600,000 crowns, in the name of the people, had nearly obtained a revocation of the decree, but TORQUEMADA interposed and prevented it. It is estimated by MARIANA that the number that quitted was 170,000 families, or about 800,000 souls. They expatriated themselves from the country which had afforded them an asylum for centuries, which they had enlightened by the learning that cast a lustre on the darkness of the age. They quitted the soil they had cultivated, the happy scenes of childhood, and the graves of their dear ones, rather than abjure the religion of their ancestors, or abandon the Law which their fathers had received at Sinai. It is estimated that, although forced to make immense sacrifices in order to realize on their property, they took with them thirty millions of ducats,* exclusive of plate, jewels, and precious stones. Those from Aragon went to Navarre; many others went to Italy and were kindly received by Pope ALEXANDER VI. at Rome, although, for this cruel act, he conferred the title of Catholic on the crown of Spain. Some went to Turkey and Africa, and the miseries they underwent have been the theme of many authors. Of those who went to Portugal, those who could pay eight crusados per head were afforded a temporary asylum, but the poorer were seized and sent to colonize their ultramarine possessions.

" 1495.—EMANUEL of Portugal appointed as his astronomer and historiographer Rabbi ABRAHAM ZACUTO, formerly professor of astronomy at Saragossa. He was the author of the chronological work *Sifar Yochsin*.

" 1496.—EMANUEL, married to the daughter of FERDINAND and ISABELLA, was instigated by them to drive the Jews from Portugal, although he had previously protected them. He appointed Viana, Oporto, and Lisbon as ports of embarkation, but afterwards confined them to Lisbon. It was ordered that children under fourteen years of age be taken from their parents and baptized, and many mothers slew their children to avoid it.

---

* "Historie der Juden," p. 509.

		1969.			
Tishri	1	First Day of New Year	Saturday	Sept.	13
"	3	Fast of Gedaliah	Monday	"	15
"	10	Yom-Kippoor	Monday	"	22
"	15	First Day of Tabernacle	Saturday	"	27
"	21	Hoshannah-Rabbah	Friday	Oct.	3
"	22	Sh'mini-Atseres................	Saturday	"	4
"	23	Simchas-Torah	Sunday	"	5
Cheshvan.		Rosh-Chodesh	Sun.-Mon.	"	12-13
Kislev	1	Rosh-Chodesh	Tuesday	Nov.	11
"	25	First Day of Chanukah	Friday	Dec.	5
Tebet	1	Rosh-Chodesh	Wednesday	"	10
"	10	Fast of Tebet	Friday	"	19
		1970.			
Sh'vat	1	Rosh-Chodesh	Thursday	Jan.	8
Adar.		Rosh-Chodesh	Fri.-Sat.	Feb.	6-7
2d Adar.		Rosh-Chodesh....	Sun -Mon.	Mar.	8-9
"	13	Fast of Esther................	Saturday*	"	21
"	14-15	Purim	Sun.-Mon.	"	22-23
Nissan	1	Rosh-Chodesh	Tuesday	April	7
"	15	First Day of Passover	Tuesday	"	21
Ivar.		Rosh-Chodesh	Wed.-Thurs.	May	6-7
"	18	Lag-B'Omer.................... 33d day of Omer.	Sunday	"	24
Sivan	1	Rosh-Chodesh	Friday	June	5
"	6	First Day of Pentecost	Wednesday	"	10
Tammuz.		Rosh-Chodesh	Sat.-Sun.	July	4-5
"	17	Fast of Tammuz................	Tuesday	"	21
Av	1	Rosh-Chodesh	Monday	Aug.	3
"	9	Fast of Av	Tuesday	"	11
Ellul.		Rosh-Chodesh	Tues.-Wed.	Sept.	1-2

* Observed Thursday previous.

EVENTFUL RECORDS.

CÆ. 655.—Caliph Omar took Jerusalem.

The capita tax levied on the Jews was abolished by Bathilda, the widow of Clovis.

" 675.—The Jews were banished from Languedoc by Wamba, King of the Goths.

" 687.—The first Arabian money was coined by a Jew, who was selected for that purpose by the Caliph Abd-el-Malik.

" 688.—Jews who embraced Christianity were, by order of the Council of Toledo, made nobles and declared free from impost.

O.Æ. 1499.—Jews banished from the city of Nuremberg.

" 1501.—Louis XII. banished them from Provence.

" 1503.—Pope Pius III. protected and favored them.

Rabbi Don Judah, son of Rabbi Don Isaac Abarbanel, author of the Philography, practised medicine successfully at Genoa.

" 1505.—At Lisbon, 3,000 New Christians were massacred. Twenty thousand families, many of them refugees from Spain and Portugal, were banished by Ferdinand on his becoming king of Naples.

" 1508.—Don Isaac Abarbanel, whose many writings are universally admired, died at Venice, at the age of 71 years. On quitting Spain, he went to Naples and became minister to Alphonso V., on whose death he filled the same office under Ferdinand II. (when Charles VIII. overran the Neapolitan territory). He accompanied the unfortunate monarch in his exile, remaining with him until his death. He then settled at Venice, where he was engaged by the Senate to assist in the formation of the treaty with Portugal regarding the trade in spices.

" 1509.—The bishopric of Cologne banished the Jews.

" 1510.—At Brandenburg, many were persecuted and murdered.

Pope Alexander VI. wrote to all the States in Italy to grant the exiles from Spain and Portugal the same privileges as resident Jews.

At the taking of Tripoli, the Jews were made captives, but ransomed by those of Naples and Rome.

" 1511.—A Hebrew printing press was set up by Daniel Bomberg.

Samuel Alvarensi, a refugee from Spain, became the favorite of Abusaid, King of Fez, who was killed and his kingdom taken by the Cherifians. Alvarensi then took command of 400 of the late king's faithful vassals, and embarked for Ceuta, which was besieged by the Cherifians; and, with this small force, surprised and attacked their army of 40,000 men, compelling them to raise the siege and return to Fez.*

" 1513.—Selim I. appointed Joseph Amon as his physician.

The Jews of Media and Persia were persecuted by Sophi Ismael.

" 1517.—By order of the Sultan, Moses Amon translated the Hebrew ritual into the Turkish language.

The celebrated Rabbi Elias Levita, a noted grammarian and lexicographer, was professor of Hebrew at Padua.

* "Nomologia," p. 306, and "Chronicas de los Xarifes."

		1970.			
Tishri	1	First Day of New Year	Thursday	Oct.	1
"	3	Fast of Gedaliah	Saturday*	"	3
"	10	Yom-Kippoor....................	Saturday	"	10
"	15	First Day of Tabernacle..........	Thursday	"	15
"	21	Hoshannah-Rabbah..............	Wednesday	"	21
"	22	Sh'mini-Atseres.................	Thursday	"	22
"	23	Simchas-Torah..................	Friday	"	23
Cheshvan.		Rosh-Chodesh....	Fri.-Sat.	"	30-31
Kislev	1	Rosh-Chodesh	Sunday	Nov.	29
"	25	First Day of Chanukah.	Wednesday	Dec.	23
Tebet.		Rosh-Chodesh	Mon.-Tues.	"	28-29
		1971.			
"	10	Fast of Tebet..................	Thursday	Jan.	7
Sh'vat	1	Rosh-Chodesh	Wednesday	"	27
Adar.		Rosh-Chodesh	Thurs.-Fri.	Feb.	25-26
"	13	Fast of Esther.............. ...	Wednesday	Mar.	10
"	14-15	Purim........................ :	Thurs.-Fri.	"	11-12
Nissan	1	Rosh-Chodesh	Saturday	"	27
"	15	First Day of Passover...........	Saturday	Apr.	10
Iyar.		Rosh-Chodesh	Sun.-Mon.	"	25-26
"	18	Lag-B'Omer...	Thursday	May	13
		33d day of Omer.			
Sivan	1	Rosh-Chodesh	Tuesday	"	25
"	6	First Day of Pentecost..........	Sunday	"	30
Tammuz.		Rosh-Chodesh	Wed.-Thurs.	June	23-24
"	17	Fast of Tammuz................	Saturday*	July	10
Av	1	Rosh-Chodesh....	Friday	"	23
"	9	Fast of Av....	Saturday*	"	31
Ellul.		Rosh-Chodesh	Sat.-Sun.	Aug.	21-22

* Observed following day.

EVENTFUL RECORDS.

C.Æ. 693.—The Jews of Africa were charged by EGICA with inciting the Moors to invade Spain, in consequence of which the Council of Toledo decreed their property forfeited, they were to be accounted slaves, and their children, on attaining the age of seven years, were taken from them to be brought up as Christians.

" 714.—The Moors, having conquered Spain, favored and protected the Jews.

" 720.—A number of Jews were forced into Christianity by the Emperor LEO III.

C.Æ. 1519.—CHARLES V. was offered 800,000 crowns by the Jews to permit their return to Spain, but Cardinal XIMENES prevented his acceptance of it.

" 1520.—Sultan SOLYMAN appointed as his physician MOSES, son of JOSEPH AMON.
The first edition of the Talmud was printed at Venice.

" 1521.—On the approach of the Turks, the Jews were ordered to quit Milan.

" 1522.—On Rhodes being taken by SOLYMAN, he granted the Jews many privileges.

" 1523.—A plunder of the Jews was begun by ACHMET, who revolted against SOLYMAN, in Egypt; but they were saved by IBRAHIM subduing him.

" 1526.—The impostor SAAVEDRA established the Inquisition at Portugal.*

" 1527.—A plague from the Grisons having spread into Italy, and many Jews from Spain and Portugal having come there by that road, they were accused of its introduction, and banished from many cities.

" 1529.—At the intercession of the nobles, the intended order of CHARLES V., for the Jews to quit Bologna, was abandoned.

" 1532.—At Sicily, Patras, Zante, and Coron, the Jews were made captives by ANDREW DORIA. Many of them were ransomed by the congregations of Italy.

" 1534.—Don PEDRO DE TOLEDO, Viceroy of Naples, appointed BENVENIDA, wife of the famous Don SAMUEL ABARBANEL, governess to his daughter LEONORA, who married COSMO DE MEDICI, Grand Duke of Tuscany.†
Jews banished from Sicily.

" 1535.—The Emperor of Morocco employed many Jews at his court.
At Tunis they were made captives. The congregations at Naples and Venice redeemed 150.

" 1739.—The Jews of Avignon received many honors and privileges from Pope PAUL III., in spite of many attempts to prejudice him against them.

" 1540.—Rabbi JOSEPH CARO flourished at Saphet. He was the author of the *Beth-Yosef* and *Shulchan-Aruch*, compendiums of Jewish laws and customs.
SOLYMAN had the walls of Jerusalem rebuilt.

---

* "Memoirs concerning the Portuguese Inquisition," p. 15.
† "Nomologia," p. 304.

		1971.		
Tishri	1	First Day of New Year	Monday	Sept.
"	3	Fast of Gedaliah..., ...	Wednesday	"
"	10	Yom-Kippoor.	Wednesday	"
"	15	First Day of Tabernacle..........	Monday	Oct.
"	21	Hoshannah-Rabbah..............	Sunday	"
"	22	Sh'mini-Atseres.	Monday	"
"	23	Simchas-Torah	Tuesday	"
Cheshvan.		Rosh-Chodesh	Tues.-Wed.	"
Kislev.		Rosh-Chodesh	Thurs.-Fri.	Nov.
"	25	First Day of Chanukah..........	Monday	Dec.
Tebet.		Rosh Chodesh	Sat.-Sun.	"
"	10	Fast of Tebet.	Tuesday	"
		1972.		
Sh'vat	1	Rosh-Chodesh	Monday	Jan.
Adar.		Rosh Chodesh	Tues.-Wed.	Feb.
"	13	Fast of Esther	Monday	"
"	14-15	Purim	Tues.-Wed.	{ Mar.
Nissan	1	Rosh-Chodesh	Thursday	"
"	15	First Day of Passover............	Thursday	"
Iyar.		Rosh-Chodesh	Fri.-Sat.	Apr.
"	18	Lag-B'Omer.................... 33d day of Omer.	Tuesday	May
Sivan	1	Rosh-Chodesh	Sunday	"
"	6	First Day of Pentecost.....	Friday	"
Tammuz.		Rosh-Chodesh	Mon.-Tues.	June
"	17	Fast of Tammuz	Thursday	"
Av	1	Rosh-Chodesh	Wednesday	July
"	9	Fast of Av	Thursday	"
Ellul.		Rosh-Chodesh	Thurs.-Fri.	Aug.

EVENTFUL RECORDS.

CÆ. 740.—English chronicles first make mention of the Jews. Chr
were prohibited by the Archbishop of York from joining
them at their festivals. BALAN, King of Cozar, bec
convert to Judaism.

" 754.—Imposts were laid on the Christians by the Caliph ABU G
FAR ALMANZOR, and he appointed Jews to collect them

" 798.—A Jew named ISAAC, and Counts SIGISMUND and LANGF
were appointed by CHARLEMAGNE as an embassy to tl
liph HAROUN AL RASCHID. During the journey th
counts died. ISAAC continued the journey alone, an

C.Æ. 1540.—The historian Rabbi GUEDALYIAH JACHIA, author of the *Shalshalas Hakabala* (traditions), was famous at Imola.

"   1541.—Jews banished from Naples by the Emperor CHARLES V.

A treaty for eight years was made with the Jews of Milan by ANDREW DORIA.

"   1543.—The Spaniards, on taking Oran, plundered the Jews and sold many as slaves.

"   1545.—Five thousand Jews, with their houses, synagogues, and libraries, were burned at Salonica.

"   1548.—The Jews at Mantua were invited by HENRY II. to settle in France.

"   1550.—At Mantua, MARGARET, the duke's mother, took their cemetery away from them.

As true subjects and denizens of HENRY II. he granted them letters patent, empowering them to purchase, inherit, and possess, undisturbed, real estate in France.

"   1553.—Pope JULIUS III. ordered the Talmud to be burned throughout Italy.

Synagogues at Pesaro were plundered and the Scrolls of the Law desecrated.

Divre Hayomim L'malach Tsorfos (the Annals of the Kings of France and Ottoman Empire), a highly valued work, was written by Rabbi JOSEPH COHEN.

"   1554.—The first party of Portuguese Jews, on going to Holland, were driven by a storm to Embden, whence they went to Amsterdam.

"   1556.—A tax of 10 ducats was levied on each synagogue by Pope PAUL IV. for the instruction of catechumens. He persecuted the Jews greatly, but repented of it afterwards, and during the sickness previous to his death said: "Whilst I live I will never hate or molest them as I have done."

JACOB CANSINO was commissioned, on several occasions, ambassador to the African States. He was appointed Spanish minister to the court of Morocco, a position filled by his family for seventy-seven years.

"   1558.—At Prague, all Hebrew books were seized; but were returned during the following year.

"   1560.—Fires, which the Jews were accused of starting, occurring in several parts of the German Empire, many of them were burned and they were banished from Prague; but were recalled the same year by the Emperor FERDINAND, the real incendiaries having been discovered.

The great commentator, Rabbi MOSES ALSHECH, noted at Saphet.

		1972.			
Tishri	1	First Day of New Year..........	Saturday	Sept.	9
"	3	Fast of Gedaliah................	Monday	"	11
"	10	Yom-Kippoor	Monday	"	18
"	15	First Day of Tabernacle	Saturday	"	23
"	21	Hoshaunah-Rabbah	Friday	"	29
"	22	Sh'mini-Atseres.................	Saturday	"	30
"	23	Simchas-Torah.................	Sunday	Oct.	1
Cheshvan.		Rosh-Chodesh	Sun.-Mon.	"	8-9
Kislev	1	Rosh-Chodesh	Tuesday	Nov.	7
"	25	First Day of Chanukah	Friday	Dec.	1
Tebet	1	Rosh-Chodesh	Wednesday	"	6
"	10	Fast of Tebet...................	Friday	"	15
		1973.			
Sh'vat	1	Rosh-Chodesh	Thursday	Jan.	4
Adar.		Rosh-Chodesh	Fri.-Sat.	Feb.	2-3
2d Adar.		Rosh-Chodesh..................	Sun.-Mon.	Mar.	4-5
"	13	Fast of Esther.................	Saturday*	"	17
"	14-15	Purim	Sun.-Mon.	"	18-19
Nissan	1	Rosh-Chodesh	Tuesday	Apr.	3
"	15	First Day of Passover...........	Tuesday	"	17
Iyar.		Rosh-Chodesh	Wed.-Thurs.	May	2-3
"	18	Lag-B'Omer................... 33d day of Omer.	Sunday	"	20
Sivan	1	Rosh-Chodesh................,.........	Friday	June	1
"	6	First Day of Pentecost.	Wednesday	"	6
Tammuz.		Rosh-Chodesh	Sat.-Sun.	" July	30 1
"	17	Fast of Tammuz................	Tuesday	"	17
Av	1	Rosh-Chodesh	Monday	"	30
"	9	Fast of Av	Tuesday	Aug.	7
Ellul.		Rosh-Chodesh	Tues.-Wed.	"	28-29

* Observed Thursday previous.

EVENTFUL RECORDS.

successful in obtaining for his sovereign the cession of Jerusalem. The Jews were thereupon ordered to be protected from all harm, and noblemen were appointed by CHARLEMAGNE to insure their safety. At Narbonne, where there were two mayors, one was always to be a Jew, in consequence of the Jewish population being very numerous.

C.Æ. 815.—AGOBARD. Bishop of Lyons, was very aggressive towards the Jews, and made many attempts to persecute them. His influence was counteracted by that of ZEDEKIAH, who was physician to LOUIS LE DEBONNAIRE.

C.Æ. 1569.—On February 26th, Pope PIUS V. ordered the Jews to quit all Papal dominions, except Rome and Ancona, under a penalty of slavery and confiscation of their property.

" 1570.—Cyprus was taken by SELIM II., who gave the Jews many privileges.

" 1571.—He sent SOLOMON ROPHÉ to negotiate a treaty of peace with Venice.

The author of *M'our Inaryim* (Light of the Eyes), Rabbi ASARIUS DE RUBIES, flourished at Ferrara.

" 1574.—At Moravia, where many Jews had been burned, the persecution of them was stopped by MAXIMILIAN II.

The synagogue at Fez, which had been destroyed, was rebuilt by MULEY MAHOMED, who appointed a Jew his prime minister and treasurer.

" 1575.—All privileges which had been granted to the Jews by HENRY II. of France were confirmed by the regency of HENRY III., and the magistrates were ordered to protect them from persecution or molestation.

Rabbi JOSEPH CARO, author of the *Shulchan-Aruch*, died.

" 1576.—SELIM II. gave permission to establish Hebrew printing presses at Constantinople and Thessalonica.

" 1578.—On assuming the throne, STEPHEN BARTHORI guaranteed to the Jews in Poland all rights and privileges which they then enjoyed.

" 1584.—On payment of a large sum, and naming the period for the coming of the Messiah, toleration was granted to the Jews of Persia by ABBAS THE GREAT. To gain time they fixed it at seventy years, whereupon he made them sign an agreement to become Moslems if their prediction did not come to pass, and pledging himself and subjects to embrace Judaism if it came true.*

" 1585.—All decrees against the Jews revoked by Pope SIXTUS V. He gave them many privileges and admitted them to all cities of the Ecclesiastical States. A monopoly of the silk trade was granted by him to Rabbi MEIR.

" 1588.—The Dutch, under General SCHENCK, plundered the Jews at Bonn.

For the gallant conduct of the Jews in defence of Prague, Emperor RUDOLPH II. tendered his thanks through Rabbi LIVA BITZLEER.

* Maynard's "Hist. of the Jews," p. 610.

5734 A.M. 1973-'74 CÆ.

		1973.			
Tishri	1	First Day of New Year	Thursday	Sept.	27
"	3	Fast of Gedaliah	Saturday*	"	29
"	10	Yom-Kippoor	Saturday	Oct.	6
"	15	First Day of Tabernacle	Thursday	"	11
"	21	Hoshannah-Rabbah	Wednesday	"	17
"	22	Sh'mini-Atseres	Thursday	"	18
"	23	Simchas-Torah	Friday	"	19
Cheshvan.		Rosh-Chodesh	Fri.-Sat.	"	26-27
Kislev.		Rosh-Chodesh	Sun.-Mon.	Nov.	25-26
"	25	First Day of Chanukah	Thursday	Dec.	20
Tebet.		Rosh-Chodesh	Tues.-Wed.	"	25-26
		1974.			
"	10	Fast of Tebet	Friday	Jan.	4
Sh'vat	1	Rosh-Chodesh	Thursday	"	24
Adar.		Rosh-Chodesh	Fri.-Sat.	Feb.	22-23
"	13	Fast of Esther	Thursday	Mar.	7
"	14-15	Purim	Fri.-Sat.	"	8-9
Nissan	1	Rosh-Chodesh	Sunday	"	24
"	15	First Day of Passover	Sunday	Apr.	7
Iyar.		Rosh-Chodesh	Mon.-Tues.	"	22-23
"	18	Lag-B'Omer (33d day of Omer.)	Friday	May	10
Sivan	1	Rosh-Chodesh	Wednesday	"	21
"	6	First Day of Pentecost	Monday	"	27
Tammuz.		Rosh-Chodesh	Thurs.-Fri.	June	20-21
"	17	Fast of Tammuz	Sunday	July	7
Av	1	Rosh-Chodesh	Saturday	"	20
"	9	Fast of Av	Sunday	"	28
Ellul.		Rosh-Chodesh	Sun.-Mon.	Aug.	18-19

* Observed following day.

EVENTFUL RECORDS.

CÆ. 820.—Several Hebrew works were translated into Arabic by order of the Caliph MAMOUN.

" 828.—At Bézieres, during Passion Week, the people stoned all Jews whom they met in the streets.

" 836.—A Hebrew dictionary was compiled by Rabbi MENACHEM BEN SARUG, a celebrated grammarian.

" 846.—Jews in Paris and Meaux were precluded from filling civil offices.

C.Æ. 1589.—At Constantinople the Janissaries put out a fire which had broken out in the Jewish quarter, but set it on fire again because their exorbitant demand for their services was not acceded to. Three thousand houses, and property valued at fifty millions of crowns, were burned.*

" 1591.—The great Kabalist, MEHRSHAL (Rabbi SOLOMON LORIA), flourished in Poland.

At Paris, ELIAS MONTALTO, physician to MARY DE MEDICI, was publicly allowed the free observance of his religion.

" 1592.—The counsellors of HENRY JULIUS, Duke of Brunswick, persuaded him to banish the Jews from the Duchy, but he soon recalled them.

" 1593.—The edict of PIUS V., by which they were only allowed to reside in the cities of Rome, Ancona, and Avignon, was renewed by CLEMENT VIII.

" 1594.—Consuls were appointed by Pope CLEMENT VIII. to adjust the frequent disputes which occurred between the Jews and the custom-house officers.

" 1595.—At Amsterdam, on the day of Atonement, the Jews were surrounded in their synagogues by an armed force, being suspected of Catholicism. The officers finding Hebrew prayer books instead of crucifixes and Catholic paraphernalia, they were allowed to remain, conditionally upon praying on every Sabbath for the prosperity of the United Provinces.

" 1598.—Jews from the Portuguese congregation at Amsterdam were the first admitted to Hamburg about this time.

" 1603.—At Hamburg, although the Catholics were not permitted to build a church, the Jews were allowed to erect a synagogue.

" 1613.—At Frankfort the magistrates discovered and frustrated a conspiracy to destroy the Jews, but it was renewed six months later. The Jewish quarter was burned and its inhabitants obliged to flee the city. Subsequently the authorities recalled them, paid them their losses, 175,900 florins, and brought them back with a military escort and music.†

The Emperor MATHIAS, in recognition of the philanthropic and generous acts of MORDECAI MAIZEL, of Prague, created him a Baron of the Roman Empire.‡

" 1615.—A rebellion broke out at Berlin, which caused the Jews to be driven out also from Frankfort and Worms, but they were kindly received in the Palatinate. When the rebellion was quelled, the duke recalled them.

* "Histoire Ecclésiastique," tom. 36, p. 300.
† Jost's "Geschichte der Israeliten," Bd. 8.
‡ Manasseh Ben Israel (Mickveh Yisroile).

		1974.			
Tishri	1	First Day of New Year...........	Tuesday	Sept.	17
"	3	Fast of Gedaliah	Thursday	"	19
"	10	Yom-Kippoor	Thursday	"	26
"	15	First Day of Tabernacle.........	Tuesday	Oct.	1
"	21	Hoshannah-Rabbah..............	Monday	"	7
"	22	Sh'mini-Atseres	Tuesday	"	8
"	23	Simchas-Torah;................	Wednesday	"	9
Cheshvan.		Rosh-Chodesh	Wed.-Thurs.	"	16-17
Kislev	1	Rosh-Chodesh	Friday	Nov.	15
"	25	First Day of Chanukah...........	Monday	Dec.	9
Tebet.		Rosh-Chodesh	Sat.-Sun.	"	14-15
"	10	Fast of Tebet.................	Tuesday	"	24
		1975.			
Sh'vat	1	Rosh-Chodesh	Monday	Jan.	13
Adar.		Rosh-Chodesh.................	Tues.-Wed.	Feb.	11-12
"	13	Fast of Esther................	Monday	"	24
"	14-15	Purim.........................	Tues.-Wed.	"	25-26
Nissan	1	Rosh-Chodesh	Thursday	Mar.	13
"	15	First Day of Passover...........	Thursday	"	27
Iyar.		Rosh-Chodesh.................	Fri.-Sat.	Apr.	11-12
"	18	Lag-B'Omer...................	Tuesday	"	29
		33d day of Omer.			
Sivan	1	Rosh-Chodesh.................	Sunday	May	11
"	6	First Day of Pentecost..........	Friday	"	16
Tammuz.		Rosh-Chodesh	Mon.-Tues.	June	9-10
"	17	Fast of Tammuz....	Thursday	"	26
Av	1	Rosh-Chodesh....	Wednesday	July	9
"	9	Fast of Av....	Thursday	"	17
Ellul.		Rosh-Chodesh.................	Thurs.-Fri.	Aug.	7-8

EVENTFUL RECORDS.

C.Æ. 853.—Jews, as well as Christians, who refused to receive the Alcoran, were subjected to great persecution by the Sultan MOTA-WAKEL.

" 877.—LOUIS II. greatly oppressed the Jews.

" 893.—It is supposed that Jews first settled in Poland about this time.

" 927.—Rabbi SADIUS, the learned commentator on the Hagiographa, flourished at Sora.

" 942.—SAADYA, the celebrated "Gaon," existed.

" 948.—At Cordova, in Spain, the first Jewish college in that country was established.

C.Æ. 1616.—The *Chizuk Amuno* (Defence of the Faith) was published by Rabbi Isaac ben Abraham at Cracow.

    Samuel Palache, ambassador from Muley Sidan to the United Provinces, died at The Hague and was buried with great pomp, Prince Maurice and many of the nobility following in the cortége.

" 1625.—Emperor Ferdinand II. created Jacob Batseba a Baron of the Roman Empire.*

" 1634.—Permission given to the Jews to settle in Switzerland.

" 1637.—Amurath IV. took Bagdad and granted the Jews many privileges.

" 1640.—A namesake of Samuel Castoel succeeded him as Governor of Cochin.†

" 1641.—The Dutch government, granting toleration at the Brazils, about six hundred Jews went there with Rabbi Isaac Aboab and Rabbi Raphael Moses D'Aguilar. Many of the New Christians residing there returned to their former religion.

" 1642.—On May 22d, Her Majesty Henrietta, Queen Consort of Charles I. of Great Britain, accompanied by the Prince of Orange, visited the Portuguese synagogue at Amsterdam and received a complimentary address from the eminent writer, Rabbi Manasseh ben Israel.

" 1643.—An exact model of the Temple of Solomon having been made by Rabbi Jacob Judah Leon, of Amsterdam, he published an elaborate description of it.

" 1646.—J. Senior Teixeira was appointed by Christina of Sweden as her agent at Hamburg.

" 1647.—G. Nunes da Costa was given letters patent of nobility by John IV. and appointed by him Portuguese consul and afterwards agent and resident at The Hague. The States General presented him with a gold chain and a medal set in diamonds, to mark their appreciation of the valuable services rendered by him to the United Provinces.‡

" 1648.—Persecution was rife in Poland under the Jesuit King, John Casimir.

" 1650.—Benjamin da Costa was the first to introduce the cultivation of the sugar cane into Martinique.§

* Manasseh ben Israel (Mickveh Yisroile).
† Barrios' "Historia Universal Judaica," p. 3.
‡ Leti's "Compendio d'elle virtue Eroiche," part 2, p. 123.
§ Grégoire, "Cultes Religieuses," tom. 3.

		1975.			
Tishri	1	First Day of New Year	Saturday	Sept.	6
"	3	Fast of Gedaliah	Monday	"	8
"	10	Yom-Kippoor	Monday	"	15
"	15	First Day of Tabernacle	Saturday	"	20
"	21	Hoshannah-Rabbah	Friday	"	26
"	22	Sh'mini-Atseres................	Saturday	"	27
"	23	Simchas-Torah	Sunday	"	28
Cheshvan.		Rosh-Chodesh	Sun.-Mon.	Oct.	5-6
Kislev.		Rosh-Chodesh	Tues.-Wed.	Nov.	4-5
"	25	First Day of Chanukah	Saturday	"	29
Tebet.		Rosh-Chodesh	Thurs.-Fri.	Dec.	4-5
"	10	Fast of Tebet	Sunday	" .	14
		1976.			
Sh'vat	1	Rosh-Chodesh	Saturday	Jan.	3
Adar.		Rosh-Chodesh	Sun.-Mon.	Feb.	1-2
2d Adar.		Rosh-Chodesh....	Tues.-Wed.	Mar.	2-3
"	13	Fast of Esther................	Monday	"	15
"	14-15	Purim.......................	Tues.-Wed.	"	16-17
Nissan	1	Rosh-Chodesh ... .,.....	Thursday	April	1
"	15	First Day of Passover	Thursday	"	15
Iyar.		Rosh-Chodesh ....·........	Fri.-Sat.	{ " 30 / May 1	
"	18	Lag-B'Omer................... *33d day of Omer.*	Tuesday	"	18
Sivan	1	Rosh-Chodesh	Sunday	"	30
"	6	First Day of Pentecost	Friday	June	4
Tammuz.		Rosh-Chodesh	Mon.-Tues.	"	28-29
"	17	Fast of Tammuz...............	Thursday	July	15
Av	1	Rosh-Chodesh	Wednesday	"	28
"	9	Fast of Av	Thursday	Aug.	5
Ellul.		Rosh-Chodesh	Thurs.-Fri.	"	26-27

EVENTFUL RECORDS.

CÆ. 980.—The colleges at Babylon were closed and many of their most learned members went to Europe. Rabbi MOSES, called "Clothed in Sackcloth," obtained great fame at Cordova. He was redeemed from pirates by his brethren, and although his identity was at that time unknown, his great learning and profound knowledge obtained for him the distinction of being made president of the college in that city.

" 1006.—The Caliph HAYSHEM directed that the *Talmud* should be translated into Arabic.

" 1012.—The Turks took possession of Jerusalem.

CÆ. 1653.—Settlement of the Jews at Surinam.

The MISHNAH, with the commentaries of MAIMONIDES and BARTENOORAH, were translated into Spanish by Rabbi JOSEPH ABENDANA. His original manuscript is in one of the libraries at Cambridge.

" 1654.—On obtaining possession of the Brazils, the Portuguese ordered the Jews to quit, but showed them kindness and consideration. The government placed at their disposal sixteen vessels to convey them and their property to any destination they chose, and furnished them with passports and safe-guards.

After abdicating and changing her religion, CHRISTINA of Sweden went to Hamburg and resided with the family of TEIXEIRA, her former agent.

" 1655.—At the invitation of Mr. Secretary THURLOE, Rabbi MANASSEH BEN ISRAEL, accompanied by several Jews, went to England and presented petitions to CROMWELL and the Parliament in behalf of their brethren. *

On the 4th of December, a council was held at Whitehall, to which Lord Chief Justice GLYNN, Lord Chief Baron STEELE, the Lord Mayor, Sheriffs, and several merchants and divines were summoned, to consider the following petition and propositions made by Rabbi MANASSEH:

"These are the graces and favors which, in the name of my Hebrew nation, I, MANASSEH BEN ISRAEL, do request of your most Serene Highness, whom God make as prosperous and give as happy success to in all the enterprises as your Serene Highness could wish and desire.

"1st. That our Hebrew nation be received and admitted into this puissant commonwealth, under the protection and safeguard of your Highness, even as the natives themselves. And for the greater security, in time to come, I supplicate your Highness to cause an oath to be given (if you should think fit) to all the heads and generals of armies to defend us on all occasions.

"2d. That it please your Highness to allow us public synagogues, not only in England, but also in other places under the power of your Highness, and to observe in all things our religion as we ought.

"3d. That we may have a place or cemetery outside of the town to bury our dead, without being troubled by any.

"4th. That we may be permitted to deal in all sorts of merchandise, the same as others.

"5th. That, to the end that those who come may be for the utility of this nation, and may live without bringing prejudice to any, and not to give offence, your most Serene Highness will make choice of some person of quality, to inform himself of and receive the passports of those who shall come in, who, upon their arrival, shall certify him thereof, and oblige themselves by oath to maintain fealty to your Highness in this land.

* Petition of Thomas Violet to Parliament

		1976.			
Tishri	1	First Day of New Year	Saturday	Sept.	25
"	3	Fast of Gedaliah...............	Monday	"	27
"	10	Yom-Kippoor....................	Monday	Oct.	4
"	15	First Day of Tabernacle.........	Saturday	"	9
"	21	Hoshannah-Rabbah.............	Friday	"	15
"	22	Sh'mini-Atseres...............	Saturday	"	16
"	23	Simchas-Torah.................	Sunday	"	17
Cheshvan.		Rosh-Chodesh	Sun.-Mon.	"	24-25
Kislev	1	Rosh-Chodesh	Tuesday	Nov.	23
"	25	First Day of Chanukah	Friday	Dec.	17
Tebet	1	Rosh-Chodesh	Wednesday	"	22
"	10	Fast of Tebet..................	Friday	"	31
		1977.			
Sh'vat	1	Rosh-Chodosh	Thursday	Jan.	20
Adar.		Rosh-Chodesh	Fri.-Sat.	Feb.	18-19
"	13	Fast of Esther.................	Thursday	Mar.	3
"	14-15	Purim..................	Fri.-Sat.	"	4-5
Nissan	1	Rosh-Chodesh .. ..·...	Sunday	"	20
"	15	First Day of Passover	Sunday	Apr.	3
Iyar.		Rosh-Chodesh	Mon.-Tues.	"	18-19
"	18	Lag-B'Omer	Friday	May	6
		33d day of Omer.			
Sivan	1	Rosh-Chodesh	Wednesday	"	18
"	6	First Day of Pentecost............	Monday	"	23
Tammuz.		Rosh-Chodesh	Thurs.-Fri.	June	16-17
"	17	Fast of Tammuz................	Sunday	July	3
Av	1	Rosh-Chodesh	Saturday	"	16
"	9	Fast of Av.....................	Sunday	"	24
Ellul.		Rosh-Chodesh	Sun.-Mon.	Aug.	14-15

EVENTFUL RECORDS.

C.Æ. 1020.—The Jews were banished from England by CANUTE. Many learued Jews left the East and went into Spain and Germany in consequence of the persecutions of GELA-LE-DOULAH in Persia.

" 1027.—ABBAS, King of Granada, selected Rabbi SAMUEL LEVY as his Prime Minister.

" 1030.—Polygamy in Christian countries was prohibited by the Jewish Synod at Worms, under direction of Rabbi GERSHON, the elder.

" 1040.—Rabbi YITZCHAK ALPHEZI, the *Alphaz*, celebrated for his erudition, was greatly famed at Cordova.

EVENTFUL RECORDS.

"6th. And to the intent that they may not be troublesome to the judges
of the land, touching the contests and differences that may arise be-
twixt those of our nation, that your most Serene Highness will give
license to the head of the synagogue to take with him two almoners of
his nation, to accord and determine all the differences and process, according to the Mosaic law, with liberty, nevertheless, to appeal from
the said sentence to the civil judges, the sum wherein the parties shall
be condemned being first deposited.

"7th. That in case there may have been any law against our Jewish
nation, that they in the first place and before all things be revoked, to
the end that by these means we may remain with greater security under
the safeguard and protection of your Serene Highness.

"Which things your most Serene Highness granting to us, we shall
always remain affectionately obliged to pray to God for the prosperity
of your Highness and of your most illustrious and sage council ; that it
will please Him to give happy success to all the undertakings of your
most Serene Highness, Amen.*

CÆ. 1655.—The council reassembled on Dec. 7th, 12th, and 14th, on which
last-mentioned day the Jews were admitted into England.
"Now were the Jews admitted." †

On the 18th December the conference concerning the propo-
sals about the admission of the Jews ended, without further
adjournment or coming to a decision. The judges declared
that there was no law which forbade the return of the Jews
into England. The divines were divided in opinion, some
asserting that the Scriptures promised their conversion.
CROMWELL therefore declared that, as there was a promise
for their conversion, means must be used to that end,
which was, preaching the Gospel, and that that could not
be done unless they were admitted where it was preached. ‡
In the end, public admission was laid aside, as decried by the
clergy, but CROMWELL and his council, on listening to de-
bates, gave a dispensation and toleration to a large number
of Jews living in London,§ and granted them permission to
build a synagogue.

1656.—The first synagogue was built by the Portuguese congregation
in King street, Duke's place, afterwards known as Bevis
Marks. ‖

A plot was leased for a term of ninety-nine years at Mile End
for a burial ground. The Spanish and Portuguese Jews'
Hospital was subsequently built thereon.

*Public Intelligencer, 17th to 24th December, and Mercurius Politicus, 20th to 27th
December, 1655.
† "Evelyn's Memoirs," vol. i., page 288.
‡ Burton's "History of Oliver Cromwell," p. 136.
§ Thos. Violet's petition.
‖ Bishop Burnett's History of his own Times, vol. i., p. 17.

		1977.			
Tishri	1	First Day of New Year	Tuesday	Sept.	13
"	3	Fast of Gedaliah	Thursday	"	15
"	10	Yom-Kippoor.	Thursday	"	22
"	15	First Day of Tabernacle.	Tuesday	"	27
"	21	Hoshannah-Rabbah..............	Monday	Oct.	3
"	22	Sh'mini-Atseres................	Tuesday	"	4
"	23	Simchas-Torah.................	Wednesday	"	5
Cheshvan.		Rosh-Chodesh	Wed.-Thurs.	"	12-13
Kislev	1	Rosh-Chodesh	Friday	Nov.	11
"	25	First Day of Chanukah	Monday	Dec.	5
Tebet.		Rosh-Chodesh...................	Sat.-Sun.	"	10-11
"	10	Fast of Tebet..................	Tuesday	"	20
		1978.			
Sh'vat	1	Rosh-Chodesh	Monday	Jan.	9
Adar.		Rosh-Chodesh	Tues.-Wed.	Feb.	7-8
2d Adar.		Rosh-Chodesh	Thurs.-Fri.	Mar.	9-10
"	13	Fast of Esther.................	Wednesday	"	22
"	14-15	Purim......	Thurs.-Fri.	"	23-24
Nissan	1	Rosh-Chodesh	Saturday	Apr.	8
"	15	First Day of Passover...........	Saturday	"	22
Iyar.		Rosh-Chodesh	Sun.-Mon.	May	7-8
"	18	Lag-B'Omer	Thursday	"	25
		33d day of Omer.			
Sivan	1	Rosh-Chodesh	Tuesday	June	6
"	6	First Day of Pentecost..........	Sunday	"	11
Tammuz.		Rosh-Chodesh	Wed.-Thurs.	July	5-6
"	17	Fast of Tammuz	Saturday*	"	22
Av	1	Rosh-Chodesh	Friday	Aug.	4
"	9	Fast of Av....................	Saturday*	"	12
Ellul.		Rosh-Chodesh	Sat.-Sun.	Sept.	2-3

* Observed following day.

EVENTFUL RECORDS.

C.Æ. 1050.—ABULCASEM, King of Granada, received instruction in mathematics from Rabbi ISAAC BEN-BAROOCH, who was famous in that science.

" 1055.—On the death of Rabbi SAMUEL LEVY, prime minister to ABBAS, King of Granada, his son JOSEPH succeeded him.

" 1062.—An uprising took place and an attempt was made by the people to murder the Jews at Castile. FERDINAND. of Castile, used his efforts to protect them. on hearing which Pope ALEXANDER II. wrote to him as follows: " What we have heard of you is much to our satisfaction. which is, that you have defended the Jews that live amongst you against those who designed to kill them."

C.Æ. **1656.**—An attempt to expel the Jews from Switzerland was frustrated by opposition from some of the cantons.

The following advertisement of the first Jewish work published in England appeared in the *Mercurius Politicus*, 7th to 14th of February : " A short Introduction to the Hebrew Tongue, the like never before published, by JOHN DAVIS. Sold by HUMPHREY MOSELY, Prince's Arms, St. Paul's Church Yard." ·

The letters patent granted to the Jews by HENRY II. in 1550 were confirmed by LOUIS XIV.

" **1657.**—The first interment in the Jewish burial ground was that of ISAAC BRITTO.

MANASSEH BEN ISRAEL, the great scholar and philanthropist, died.

" **1659.**—A charter for the colonization of the island of Cayenne was granted to DAVID NASSY and other Portuguese Jews by the Dutch West India Company.*

" **1660.**—On January 18th, the king and Parliament were petitioned by THOMAS VIOLET, a goldsmith, to order the Jews to quit · England and to confiscate their property.

" **1662.**—The Portuguese synagogue was visited by THOMAS GREEN-HALGH, where he found upward of one hundred men and many richly attired ladies.†

" **1664.**—The Dutch inhabitants and the Jews forced to quit Cayenne by the French when they took the island. The Jews went to Surinam.

The Jews, being threatened with insecurity and attacks against their persons and properties, petitioned King CHARLES II., who on August 22d declared, by an order in Council, that, " as long as they demean themselves peaceably and with due submission to the laws, they may promise themselves the effects of the same favor as formerly."

" **1665.**—By proclamation, August 17th, the British government at Surinam ratified all former privileges of the Jews, guaranteed them full enjoyment and free exercise of their religious rites and usages, and made void any summons served upon them on their Sabbaths or holidays. They were not to be called for any public duties on those days, except in urgent cases. Civil cases of less value than 10,000 pounds of sugar were to be decided by their Elders, and the magistrates were obliged to enforce their judgment. They were also per-

---

* " Essai Historique sur la Colonie de Surinam," p. 118.
† Manuscript in the Harleian Collection.

		1978.			
Tishri	1	First Day of New Year	Monday	Oct.	2
"	3	Fast of Gedaliah................	Wednesday	"	4
"	10	Yom-Kippoor	Wednesday	"	11
"	15	First Day of Tabernacle	Monday	"	16
"	21	Hoshannah-Rabbah	Sunday	"	22
"	22	Sh'mini-Atseres..........	Monday	"	23
"	23	Simchas-Torah	Tuesday	"	24
Cheshvan.		Rosh-Chodesh	Tues.-Wed.	{ " Nov.	31 1
Kislev.		Rosh-Chodesh	Thurs.-Fri.	{ " Dec.	30 1
"	25	First Day of Chanukah	Monday	"	25
Tebet.		Rosh-Chodesh	Sat.-Sun.	"	30-31
		1979.			
"	10	Fast of Tebet	Tuesday	Jan.	9
Sh'vat	1	Rosh-Chodesh ...'...............	Monday	"	29
Adar.		Rosh-Chodesh	Tues.-Wed.	Feb.	27-28
"	13	Fast of Esther..................	Monday	Mar.	12
"	14-15	Purim	Tues.-Wed.	"	13-14
Nissan	1	Rosh-Chodesh	Thursday	"	29
"	15	First Day of Passover	Thurs. Fri.	Apr.	12-13
Iyar.		Rosh-Chodesh	Fri.-Sat.	"	27-28
"	18	Lag-B'Omer ... . 33d day of Omer.	Tuesday	May	15
Sivan	1	Rosh-Chodesh	Sunday	"	27
"	6	First Day of Pentecost	Friday	June	1
Tammuz.		Rosh-Chodesh	Mon.-Tues.	"	25-26
"	17	Fast of Tammuz....	Thursday	July	12
Av	1	Rosh-Chodesh	Wednesday	"	25
"	9	Fast of Av	Thursday	Aug.	2
Ellul.		Rosh-Chodesh	Thurs.-Fri.	"	23-24

EVENTFUL RECORDS.

C.Æ. 1062.—At this time, at Lunel, the great commentator RASHI, flourished.

" 1064.—Fifteen hundred wealthy Jewish families were plundered, in consequence of a fanatic named JUDAH HALEVI attempting to convert the Moors to Judaism. Rabbi JOSEPH LEVI, the prime minister, was executed through the jealousy and influence of the nobles.

" 1065.—The French bishops were thus addressed by Pope ALEXANDER II.: "We learn with pleasure that you have protected the Jews, that they were not killed by those going against the Saracens in Spain."

mitted to bequeath their property according to their own law of inheritance. They were given ten acres of land for the erection of a synagogue and such buildings as the congregation might need; and, in order to induce Jews to settle there, it was declared that all who came for that purpose should be considered as British-born subjects, in return for obeying all decrees of the King of England which did not infringe on their privileges.*

C.Æ. 1666.—SABBATHAI Z'VEE, the impostor, claimed to be the MESSIAH. A persecution commenced against the Jews in Persia, and continued for three years.

" 1667.—MULEY ARCHEY plundered a Jew of £400,000 to carry on his rebellion, and, in return for the success which he attained thereby, granted to the Jews of Morocco many privileges.

Surinam being again taken by the Dutch, they confirmed all privileges which the Jews then had, and entitled them to equal rights with Dutch-born subjects.

For a correct and beautiful edition of the Hebrew Bible, JOSEPH ATHIAS was presented with a gold chain by the States General of Holland.

At Amsterdam, Rabbi DAVID COHEN DE LARA published part of his Rabbinical Talmudical Lexicon called *Kesher K'Hunah* (Crown of Priesthood), with the meaning of each word, in the Chaldean, Syriac, Arabic, Persian, Turkish, Greek, Latin, Italian, French, Spanish, Portuguese, German, Saxon, and English languages. At his death, after a labor of forty years, he had got only as far as YOD, the tenth letter.

" 1669.—Whilst crossing the bridge at Leopoldstadt, ESTHER, a Jewess, the favorite mistress of LEOPOLD I., was shot. On suspicion of the act being committed by the Jews, they were banished from Vienna.

Jews were banished from Oran.

" 1670.—Many Jews quitted Surinam with the English, when it was finally ceded to the Dutch, and settled in Jamaica and other West India Islands.

LOUIS XIV. confirmed to them all the privileges formerly enjoyed at Metz.

Persia accorded them toleration and liberty of conscience.

* " Essai Historique sur la Colonie de Surinam," p. 123.

		1979.			
Tishri	1	First Day of New Year..........	Saturday	Sept.	22
"	3	Fast of Gedaliah................	Monday	"	24
"	10	Yom-Kippoor	Monday	Oct.	1
"	15	First Day of Tabernacle	Saturday	"	6
"	21	Hoshannah-Rabbah	Friday	"	12
"	22	Sh'mini-Atseres................	Saturday	"	13
"	23	Simchas-Torah	Sunday	"	14
Cheshvan.		Rosh-Chodesh	Sun.-Mon.	"	21-22
Kislev.		Rosh-Chodesh	Tues.-Wed.	Nov.	20-21
"	25	First Day of Chanukah	Saturday	Dec.	15
Tebet.		Rosh-Chodesh	Thurs -Fri.	"	20-21
"	10	Fast of Tebet	Sunday	"	30
		1980.			
Sh'vat	1	Rosh-Chodesh	Saturday	Jan.	19
Adar.		Rosh-Chodesh	Sun. Mon.	Feb.	17-18
"	13	Fast of Esther.................	Saturday*	Mar.	1
"	14-15	Purim	Sun.-Mon.	"	2-3
Nissan	1	Rosh-Chodesh	Tuesday	"	18
"	15	First Day of Passover....	Tuesday	Apr.	1
Iyar.		Rosh-Chodesh	Wed.-Thurs.	"	16-17
"	18	Lag-B'Omer....................	Sunday	May	4
		33d day of Omer.			
Sivan	1	Rosh-Chodesh	Friday	"	16
"	6	First Day of Pentecost..........	Wednesday	"	21
Tammuz.		Rosh-Chodesh	Sat.-Sun.	June	14-15
"	17	Fast of Tammuz	Tuesday	July	1
Av	1	Rosh-Chodesh	Monday	"	14
"	9	Fast of Av	Tuesday	"	22
Ellul.		Rosh-Chodesh	Tues.-Wed.	Aug.	12-13

* Observed Thursday previous.

EVENTFUL RECORDS.

CÆ. 1066.—A number of Jews returned to England with WILLIAM THE CONQUEROR.

" 1068.—Only one burial ground was permitted them for all England, and was situated where Jewin Street, in the city of London, is now built.

" 1070.—Rabbi SOLOMON BEN GAVRIEL, the great poet, was noted at Saragossa. As specimens of his genius and beauty of style, his poems of the AZHOROS (*precepts*) and KASAR MOLCHOOS (*Ptolemaic Planetary System*) are unsurpassed.

C.Æ. 1670.—EMANUEL BELMONTE was accredited to the United Provinces as agent for Spain, and the Spanish ambassador was instructed to consult him on all matters of importance. In recognition of faithful and valuable services, CHARLES II. of Spain created him BARON DE BELMONTE. He was greatly esteemed by the various allies for the valuable assistance he rendered them.*

F. LOPES SUASSO was likewise created, by CHARLES II., BARON D'AVERNA for similar services.†

" 1673.—The assassins of ESTHER being discovered, the Jews were readmitted to Vienna.

At London they were indicted for meeting for public worship, and they petitioned the king that time be given them to withdraw from his kingdom, or that they might remain unmolested. On February 11th, he ordered, in Council, "that the Attorney General stop all proceedings, and that they receive no further trouble in this behalf."

" 1677.—BARUCH SPINOZA, the celebrated philosopher, died.

" 1683.—Jews ordered to evacuate the French colonies.

" 1684.—A treaty for MULEY ISMAEL was concluded with the United Provinces by JOSEPH DE TOLEDO.

" 1685.—Under Statute 23d of ELIZABETH, writs were issued and several Jewish merchants were arrested on the Exchange for not attending any church; upon which they appealed to the king for his protection and permission to follow their own religious observances. On November 13th, it was ordered in Council "that the Attorney General do stop all the said proceedings, His Majesty's intention being that they should not be troubled on this account, but that they should quietly enjoy the full exercise of their religion whilst they behave themselves dutifully and obediently to his government." There were present at this council: The King's Most Excellent Majesty; H. R. H. PRINCE GEORGE; Archbishop of Canterbury, Bishop of London; The Lords Chancellor, Treasurer, Privy Seal, and Chamberlain; The Dukes of Ormond and Queensbury; The Earls of Huntingdon, Bridgewater, Birkley, Nottingham, Plymouth, Craven, Peterborough, Middleton, Sunderland, Morray; Viscounts Fauconberg, Preston, Melfort; Lords Dartmouth and Godolphin and the Chancellor of the Exchequer.

* Leti's "Compendio dello virtu Eroiche," part 2, page 124.
† Ibid.

		1980.			
Tishri	1	First Day of New Year	Thursday	Sept.	11
"	3	Fast of Gedaliah	Saturday*	"	13
"	10	Yom-Kippoor	Saturday	"	20
"	15	First Day of Tabernacle	Thursday	"	25
"	21	Hoshaunah-Rabbah	Wednesday	Oct.	1
"	22	Sh'mini-Atseres	Thursday	"	2
"	23	Simchas-Torah	Friday	"	3
Cheshvan.		Rosh-Chodesh	Fri.-Sat.	"	10-11
Kislev	1	Rosh-Chodesh	Sunday	Nov.	9
"	25	First Day of Chanukah	Wednesday	Dec.	3
Tebet	1	Rosh-Chodesh	Monday	"	8
"	10	Fast of Tebet	Wednesday	"	17
		1981.			
Sh'vat	1	Rosh-Chodesh	Tuesday	Jan.	6
Adar.		Rosh-Chodesh	Wed.-Thurs.	Feb.	4-5
2d Adar.		Rosh-Chodesh	Fri.-Sat.	Mar.	6-7
"	13	Fast of Esther	Thursday	"	19
"	14-15	Purim	Fri.-Sat.	"	20-21
Nissan	1	Rosh-Chodesh	Sunday	Apr.	5
"	15	First Day of Passover	Sunday	"	19
Iyar.		Rosh-Chodesh	Mon.-Tues.	May	4-5
"	18	Lag-B'Omer	Friday	"	22
		33d day of Omer.			
Sivan	1	Rosh Chodesh	Wednesday	June	3
"	6	First Day of Pentecost	Monday	"	8
Tammuz.		Rosh-Chodesh	Thurs.-Fri.	July	2-3
"	17	Fast of Tammuz	Sunday	"	19
Av	1	Rosh-Chodesh	Saturday	Aug.	1
"	9	Fast of Av	Sunday	"	9
Ellul.		Rosh-Chodesh	Sun.-Mon.	"	30 31

* Observed following day.

EVENTFUL RECORDS.

C.Æ. 1080.—ALPHONSO I. of Castile afforded protection to the Jews and conferred many honorable and responsible positions upon them.

" 1086.—Rabbi NATHAN, author of the *Arooch* (Talmudical Lexicon), was famous at Rome.

" 1096.—The so-called holy wars were begun by the Crusaders, who murdered such Jews as would not consent to be baptized. In Aragon and Navarre there were many martyrs, but the most cruel butchery was in Germany. Men and women slew

C.Æ. 1685.—The Jews who had been made prisoners in the Morea by General Morosini were released by the Republic of Venice, through the intercession of Pope Innocent XI.

In the French colonies, all Jews found there were ordered to be seized and their property confiscated.

" 1687.—Peter the Great excluded the Jews from Russia.

" 1690.—William III. rejected a petition from the Council at Jamaica that Jews be ordered to quit that island.

" 1692.—At Broad Court, Duke's Place, the first German synagogue in London was built. It is now the site of the Great Synagogue in that city.

" 1696.—At Oxford, an almanac was printed with a daily Christian calendar on one side and a Jewish one opposite.

" 1697.—Alexander Nunez da Costa succeeded to his father's posts and honors, although powerful influence was used by several parties to obtain those offices.

" 1701.—The Portuguese congregation in London appointed as their Chief Rabbi the learned Rabbi David Nieto, author of the work *Mattai-Dan*.

" 1709.—The royal arms of Prussia, surmounted by a crown, were engraved upon a diamond of twenty-five carats for Frederick I. by Levin Joseph, the celebrated engraver at Berlin.

" 1712.—The giving of an island in the Archipelago to the Jews, for the establishment of an independent State, was proposed by the Marquis of Langallerie.*

" 1723.—The right of Jews to hold real estate was confirmed to them by Louis XV., to which he added the words, "without their being obliged to take out letters of naturalization."

First acknowledgment of Jews as British subjects by the following act of Parliament: "Whenever any of His Majesty's subjects professing the Jewish religion shall present themselves to take the oath of abjuration, the words, 'on the true faith of a Christian,' shall be omitted out of the said oath; and the taking of it by such persons professing the Jewish religion, without the words aforesaid, in the manner as Jews are admitted to be sworn to give evidence in courts of justice, shall be deemed a sufficient taking."

" 1728.—The first Jewish synagogue in America established in New York.

" 1730.—Emperor Charles VI., King of Denmark, created Moses Lopez Pereira, Baron D'Aguilar, and he was appointed treasurer to the Empress, as Queen of Bohemia.

* Grégoire's "Cultes Religieuses," tom. 3.

1981.

Tishri	1	First Day of New Year	Tuesday	Sept.	29
"	3	Fast of Gedaliah	Thursday	Oct.	1
"	10	Yom-Kippoor	Thursday	"	8
"	15	First Day of Tabernacle	Tuesday	"	13
"	21	Hoshannah-Rabbah	Monday	"	19
"	22	Sh'mini-Atseres	Tuesday	"	20
"	23	Simchas-Torah	Wednesday	"	21
Cheshvan.		Rosh-Chodesh	Wed.-Thurs.	"	28-29
Kislev	1	Rosh-Chodesh	Friday	Nov.	27
"	25	First Day of Chanukah	Monday	Dec.	21
Tebet.		Rosh-Chodesh	Sat.-Sun.	"	26-27

1982.

"	10	Fast of Tebet	Tuesday	Jan.	5
Sh'vat	1	Rosh-Chodesh	Monday	"	25
Adar.		Rosh-Chodesh	Tues.-Wed.	Feb.	23-24
"	13	Fast of Esther	Monday	Mar.	8
"	14-15	Purim	Tues.-Wed.	"	9-10
Nissan	1	Rosh-Chodesh	Thursday	"	25
"	15	First Day of Passover	Thursday	Apr.	8
Iyar.		Rosh-Chodesh	Fri.-Sat.	"	23-24
"	18	Lag-B'Omer. 33d day of Omer.	Tuesday	May	11
Sivan	1	Rosh-Chodesh	Sunday	"	23
"	6	First Day of Pentecost	Friday	"	28
Tammuz.		Rosh-Chodesh	Mon.-Tues.	June	21-22
"	17	Fast of Tammuz	Thursday	July	8
Av	1	Rosh-Chodesh	Wednesday	"	21
"	9	Fast of Av	Thursday	"	29
Ellul.		Rosh-Chodesh	Thurs.-Fri.	Aug.	19-20

EVENTFUL RECORDS.

each other, and parents killed their children to escape the inhuman atrocities of the fiendish bigots of Spires, Metz, Cologne, Presburg, and Prague. Over two hundred who leaped into the Rhine were drawn from it to be cruelly slain. In justice to the bishops, it must be stated that they did all in their power to allay the barbarities, and many were released through their influence.

C.Æ. 1097.—Jews who had been forcibly baptized were authorized by HENRY IV. of Germany to return to their faith.

" 1105.—RASHI, the celebrated commentator, died.

C.Æ. 1735.—CHARLES, Duke of Wirtemberg, appointed SÜSZ OPPENHEIM his finance minister. The harsh conduct of the latter towards the people caused them to ill-treat the Jews.

" 1736.—The formation of an independent establishment for the Jews was proposed by the Duke of Ripperda.*

" 1738.—The Jews of Copenhagen formed a society, giving premiums to those who learned trades, in acknowledgment of CHRISTIAN VI., King of Denmark, affording them the facilities of becoming manufacturers.

" 1740.—CHARLES II. invited a return of the Jews to Naples and Sicily.
An English act of Parliament was enacted as follows : "That those Jews who had already resided in the American colonies, or who have served as mariners during the war, two years in British ships, are become natural-born subjects of Great Britain, without taking the Sacrament."

" 1749.—On June 11th, M. J. PEREIRA, interpreter at the Royal Library at Paris, explained his method of instructing the deaf and dumb, which was afterwards adopted by L'ABBÉ L'EPÉE with marked success.

" 1750.—The repeating reflecting circle, to rectify astronomical observations, was invented by TOBIAS MEYER, professor of mathematics at Göttingen.
MOSES MENDELSOHN, the great philosopher, flourished.
The Emperor of Morocco commissioned a Jew as ambassador to Denmark.
FREDERICK II. tolerated the Jews in Prussia, but on the most intolerant conditions.
For the active zeal of MOSES NAAR and GABRIEL DE LA FATTE in suppressing a revolt of the negroes at Surinam, they were presented with silver cups and the thanks of the government.†

" 1753.—The Duke of Lorraine levied a capitation tax and laid several restrictions upon the Jews.
England passed the Naturalization Bill.

" 1754.—Petitions from the city of London and other places caused its repeal.
Jewish marriages declared not to be affected by the marriage act.
ELIAS DE PAZ bequeathed twelve hundred pounds for founding a *Yeshibah* (Jewish college). It was claimed to be for superstitious purposes, and confiscated to the Crown. It was given by GEORGE II. to the Foundling Hospital.

* Grégoire's "Cultes Religieuses," tom. 3.
† "Essai Historique sur la Colonie de Surinam," p. 123.

		1982.			
Tishri	1	First Day of New Year.........	Saturday	Sept.	18
"	3	Fast of Gedaliah...............	Monday	"	20
"	10	Yom-Kippoor..................	Monday	"	27
"	15	First Day of Tabernacle	Saturday	Oct.	2
"	21	Hoshannah-Rabbah	Friday	"	8
"	22	Sh'mini-Atseres...............	Saturday	"	9
"	23	Simchas-Torah	Sunday	"	10
Cheshvan.		Rosh-Chodesh	Sun.-Mon.	"	17-18
Kislev.		Rosh-Chodesh	Tues.-Wed.	Nov.	16-17
"	25	First Day of Chanukah	Saturday	Dec.	11
Tebet.		Rosh-Chodesh	Thurs.-Fri.	"	16-17
"	10	Fast of Tebet	Sunday	"	26
		1983.			
Sh'vat	1	Rosh-Chodesh	Saturday	Jan.	15
Adar.		Rosh-Chodesh	Sun.-Mon.	Feb.	13-14
"	13	Fast of Esther.................	Saturday*	"	26
"	14-15	Purim	Sun.-Mon.	"	27-28
Nissan	1	Rosh-Chodesh	Tuesday	Mar.	15
"	15	First Day of Passover....	Tuesday	"	29
Iyar.		Rosh-Chodesh	Wed.-Thurs.	Apr.	13-14
"	18	Lag-B'Omer.................. 33d day of Omer.	Sunday	May	1
Sivan	1	Rosh-Chodesh	Friday	"	13
"	6	First Day of Pentecost..........	Wednesday	"	18
Tammuz.		Rosh-Chodesh	Sat.-Sun.	June	11-12
"	17	Fast of Tammuz	Tuesday	"	28
Av	1	Rosh-Chodesh	Monday	July	11
"	9	Fast of Av	Tuesday	"	19
Ellul.		Rosh-Chodesh	Tues.-Wed.	Aug.	9-10

* Observed Thursday previou

EVENTFUL RECORDS.

CÆ. 1111.—A Jew was appointed by COLOMANUS, Duke of Bohemia, to be his treasurer, but was afterwards banished by him through popular force and clamor.

" 1126.—A Jewish physician was called to attend LOTHARIO II. of Germany, and cured him.

" 1129.—The Jews were accorded the same rights as other citizens by ROGER of Naples, when he made Messina a residence of royalty.

" 1142.—Jews were appointed as tax collectors to ALPHONSO VII., upon his defeat of the Moors, but were driven out and banished from Tangiers.

C.Æ. 1762.—Toleration of the Jews by CATHARINE of Russia. Those of the Crimea and the Ukraine already had the protection of the government.

" 1772.—The English government passed an act that Jews should be entitled to all rights and privileges of British subjects after seven years' residence in any of its colonies.

" 1778.—General WASHINGTON constituted Colonel DAVID FRANKS his confidential aid.

" 1780.—Deputies were sent to LOUIS XVI. by the Jews of Metz with a petition to repeal all ordinances against them.

The following advantages were accorded the Jews by Emperor JOSEPH II.: All schools and universities of the Empire were to be open to them, with the right to take degrees in philosophy, medicine, and civil law. They were allowed to establish manufactories and follow any trade, except the making of gunpowder. They were under the same law as Christians, and permitted to attend fairs in towns where they did not reside.

" 1781.—For gallant conduct in an action off the Doggerbank on August 5th, the States of Holland presented a gold medal to J. D'ALMEIDA.

" 1783.—A universal language, said to be superior to the Pasigraphy, was invented by ZALKIN HOURWITZ, interpreter at the Royal Library in Paris. He also gained a prize at Metz for a memorial in favor of the Jews.

" 1784.—The oppressive laws against the Jews, by the DUKE OF LORRAINE, were revoked by LOUIS XVI.

" 1786.—MOSES MENDELSOHN, the celebrated philosopher and Bible commentator, died.

" 1788.—A commission having been appointed to remodel all laws concerning the Jews, on principles of justice, MALESHERBES was made President thereof.

" 1789.—Denmark opened to the Jews all the privileges of corporations.

ELIAS LEVY, made minister to the Emperor of Morocco, was disgraced and sold to a slave dealer at Tunis, but afterwards was redeemed and reinstated in his position.

" 1790.—Rights of citizenship claimed by the Jews of France.

The Emperor of Morocco had SOLOMON HASSAN, Spanish Consul at Tetuan, beheaded for informing his government of the intended attack on Ceuta.

" 1791.—M. BERR-ISAAC-BERR, of Nancy, published his celebrated letter.

1983.

Tishri	1	First Day of New Year	Thursday	Sept.	8
"	3	Fast of Gedaliah................	Saturday*	"	10
"	10	Yom-Kippoor...................	Saturday	"	17
"	15	First Day of Tabernacle.........	Thursday	"	22
"	21	Hoshannah-Rabbah.............	Wednesday	"	28
"	22	Sh'mini-Atseres.	Thursday	"	29
"	23	Simchas-Torah.................	Friday	"	30
Cheshvan.		Rosh-Chodesh	Fri.-Sat.	Oct.	7-8
Kislev.		Rosh-Chodesh	Sun.-Mon.	Nov.	6-7
"	25	First Day of Chanukah.........	Thursday	Dec.	1
Tebet.		Rosh-Chodesh	Tues.-Wed.	"	6-7
"	10	Fast of Tebet...................	Friday	"	16

1984.

Sh'vat	1	Rosh-Chodesh	Thursday	Jan.	5
Adar.		Rosh Chodesh	Fri.-Sat.	Feb.	3-4
2d Adar.		Rosh-Chodesh	Sun.-Mon.	Mar.	4-5
"	13	Fast of Esther	Saturday†	"	17
"	14-15	Purim	Sun.-Mon.	"	18-19
Nissan	1	Rosh-Chodesh	Tuesday	Apr.	3
"	15	First Day of Passover..........	Tuesday	"	17
Iyar.		Rosh-Chodesh	Wed.-Thurs.	May	2-3
"	18	Lag-B'Omer....................	Sunday	"	20
		33d day of Omer.			
Sivan	1	Rosh-Chodesh	Friday	June	1
"	6	First Day of Pentecost.....	Wednesday	"	6
Tammuz.		Rosh-Chodesh	Sat.-Sun.	{ " July	30 1
"	17	Fast of Tammuz	Tuesday	"	17
Av	1	Rosh-Chodesh	Monday	"	30
"	9	Fast of Av	Tuesday	Aug.	7
Ellul.		Rosh-Chodesh	Tues.-Wed.	"	28-29

*Observed following day.   † Observed Thursday previous.

EVENTFUL RECORDS.

C.Æ. 1146.—A second crusade being determined on and organized, St. Bernard, with the view of preventing a repetition of the cruel atrocities of the previous one, wrote as follows to the Archbishop of Metz: "Take thou heed that thou speak to the Jews neither good nor bad; they are not to be massacred nor persecuted, nor should you even banish them." Many were, however, killed in Germany in spite of this order, while the clergy and authorities afforded protection to those who escaped to the fortresses and castles, in which they guarded them.

C.Æ. 1792.—In the army at Praga for the defence of Warsaw, there were six battalions of Jews.*

" 1794.—On behalf of Poland's independence, a regiment of cavalry, composed entirely of Jews, fought under the leadership of KOSCIUSKO.

The Emperor of Morocco sent J. II. SUMBAL to London as envoy.

" 1795.—Jews were given the same rights as other citizens by the Batavian Republic.

" 1796.—In South Carolina LEVY MYERS became a member of the Legislature.

At Dessau the public schools were opened to the Jews.

" 1798.—M. DA COSTA ATHIAS was made President, and DR. LEMON and M. C. ASSER appointed members of the National Convention of the Batavian Republic.

" 1800.—In Denmark the public schools and universities were opened to the Jews.

" 1801.—A suggestion was made by a Society of Dutch Jews for a general congress at Lunéville of representatives of all congregations in Europe.

A Hebrew college was established at Seezen, in Germany, by M. ISRAEL JACOBSON, who was Privy Councillor to the Duke of Brunswick-Lunenburg.

" 1804.—In Switzerland there was a renewal of prohibitory laws against the Jews.

At Amsterdam, M. J. D. MEYER was made judge of the Tribunal de Première Instance and member of the Provincial State.

In Poland, Jews were prohibited from peddling.

" 1805.—The British Government sent AARON CARDOZA as envoy to the Bey of Oran, with whom he concluded a treaty on November 5th.

In Russia the Jews were authorized by Emperor ALEXANDER to work at various trades.

" 1806.—May 30th. A meeting of the Jewish deputies from the French departments was convened by the Emperor NAPOLEON.

July 26th. The first meeting was held. The minister, finding · that he had unthinkingly fixed it on the Sabbath, proposed to adjourn it, but the deputies declined his offer, stating that Jewish law commanded prompt obedience to the sovereign of the country which afforded them its protection.

* Grégoire's " Cultes Religieuses," tom. 3.

		1984.			
Tishri	1	First Day of New Year..........	Thursday	Sept.	27
"	3	Fast of Gedaliah..............	Saturday*	"	29
"	10	Yom-Kippoor.................	Saturday	Oct.	6
"	15	First Day of Tabernacle.........	Thursday	"	11
"	21	Hoshannah-Rabbah.............	Wednesday	"	17
"	22	Sh'mini Atseres....	Thursday	"	18
"	23	Simchas-Torah.................	Friday	"	19
Cheshvan.		Rosh-Chodesh.................	Fri.-Sat.	"	26-27
Kislev	1	Rosh-Chodesh.................	Sunday	Nov.	25
"	25	First Day of Chanukah..........	Wednesday	Dec.	19
Tebet.		Rosh-Chodesh.................	Mon.-Tues.	"	24-25
		1985.			
"	10	Fast of Tebet.................	Thursday	Jan.	3
Sh'vat	1	Rosh-Chodesh.................	Wednesday	"	23
Adar.		Rosh-Chodesh.................	Thurs.-Fri.	Feb.	21-22
"	13	Fast of Esther.................	Wednesday	Mar.	6
"	14-15	Purim........................	Thurs.-Fri.	"	7-8
Nissan	1	Rosh-Chodesh....	Saturday	"	23
"	15	First Day of Passover...........	Saturday	Apr.	6
Iyar.		Rosh-Chodesh.................	Sun.-Mon.	"	21-22
"	18	Lag-B'Omer...................	Thursday	May	9
		33d day of Omer.			
Sivan	1	Rosh-Chodesh.................	Tuesday	"	21
"	6	First Day of Pentecost..........	Sunday	"	26
Tammuz.		Rosh-Chodesh.................	Wed.-Thurs.	June	19-20
"	17	Fast of Tammuz....	Saturday*	July	6
Av	1	Rosh-Chodesh....	Friday	"	19
"	9	Fast of Av....	Saturday*	"	27
Ellul.		Rosh-Chodesh.................	Sat.-Sun.	Aug.	17-18

Observed following day.

EVENTFUL RECORDS.

C.Æ. 1147.—Debts to the Jews, by the Crusaders, were annulled by order of Louis VII.

The renowned rabbi, ABEN EZRA, was in the zenith of his fame. In addition to his learned commentaries on the Bible, he wrote valuable works on grammar, moral philosophy, mathematics, geometry, algebra, and astronomy; he is likewise credited with the invention of the Ecliptic.* -

The grand poet-rabbi, YEHUDAH HALEVI, is said to have existed about this period. He was the author of *Cuzri* and

* "Biblioteca Espagnola," vol. i., p. 21.

C.Æ. 1806.—September 18th. The minister proposed that all congregations in Europe be invited to send deputies, for the purpose of establishing a Grand Sanhedrin.

September 26th. Invitations issued accordingly to all the synagogues in Europe.

December 9th. Consistories established in France, and adopted since in other countries.

The Prince of Parma and Piombino put the Jews upon an equality with his other subjects.

" 1807.—The Emperor NAPOLEON decorated Rabbi ABRAHAM COLOGNA with the order of the Iron Crown.

M. C. ASSER appointed referendary to the Council of State.

In Canada, EZEKIEL HART was returned as a member of the House of Assembly. In an attempt to secure an additional partisan of their own body, the French party moved and carried his exclusion on religious grounds. The governor dissolved the House, and Mr. HART was returned again on its re-formation.

" 1808.—The order and title of Knight of the Westphalian Crown was conferred upon ISRAEL JACOBSON, Privy Councillor to the Duke of Mecklenburg. The capitation tax was rescinded in many parts of Germany upon Mr. JACOBSON'S representations.

Many restrictions were removed, and the Jews admitted to fill public offices in Westphalia.

The royal dukes visited the great German synagogue in Duke's Place, London.

The valuable cabinet of Dr. BLOCH incorporated with the Berlin Museum. His work on Ichthyology is highly esteemed and greatly prized.

A petition was presented to the Russian Government by NAHUM FUNKALSTEIN, of Sklow, to establish colonies in Nicolajow. As an encouragement, the government exempted all those who settled there from all services and military taxes for twenty years. The colonists engaged industriously in agriculture, built several villages and gave them Hebrew names, such as *Nohor-Tov* (Good River), *Yefy-Nohor* (Beautiful River), *Eer-M'nucho* (City of Rest), etc.*

" 1809.—All Jewish disabilities removed by the Grand Duke of Baden.

LOUIS, King of Holland, knighted Dr. CAPPADOCE and D. MEYER; they were also created members of the Legion of Honor by the Emperor NAPOLEON, and the King of the Belgians conferred upon them the Order of the Belgic Lion.

* Jost's " Geschichte der Israeliten," Bd. 9.

1985.

Tishri	1	First Day of New Year	Monday	Sept.	16
"	3	Fast of Gedaliah	Wednesday	"	18
"	10	Yom-Kippoor...................	Wednesday	"	25
"	15	First Day of Tabernacle.........	Monday	"	30
"	21	Hoshannah-Rabbah.............	Sunday	Oct.	6
"	22	Sh'mini-Atseres................	Monday	"	7
"	23	Simchas-Torah.................	Tuesday	"	8
Cheshvan.		Rosh-Chodesh....	Tues.-Wed.	"	15-16
Kislev	1	Rosh-Chodesh	Thursday	Nov.	14
"	25	First Day of Chanukah..........	Sunday	Dec.	8
Tebet	1	Rosh-Chodesh	Friday	"	13
"	10	Fast of Tebet.................	Sunday	"	22

1986.

Sh'vat	1	Rosh-Chodesh	Saturday	Jan.	11
Adar.		Rosh-Chodesh	Sun.-Mon.	Feb.	9-10
2d Adar.		Rosh-Chodesh	Tues.-Wed.	Mar.	11-12
"	13	Fast of Esther............... ...	Monday	"	24
"	14-15	Purim........................	Tues.-Wed.	"	25-26
Nissan	1	Rosh-Chodesh	Thursday	Apr.	10
"	15	First Day of Passover...........	Thursday	"	24
Iyar.		Rosh-Chodesh	Fri.-Sat.	May	9-10
"	18	Lag-B'Omer...................	Tuesday	"	27
		33d day of Omer.			
Sivan	1	Rosh-Chodesh	Sunday	June	8
"	6	First Day of Pentecost..........	Friday	"	13
Tammuz.		Rosh-Chodesh	Mon.-Tues.	July	7 8
"	17	Fast of Tammuz................	Thursday	"	24
Av	1	Rosh-Chodesh....	Wednesday	Aug.	6
"	9	Fast of Av....	Thursday	"	14
Ellul.		Rosh-Chodesh	Thurs.-Fri.	Sept.	4-5

EVENTFUL RECORDS.

many other valuable works and poems. The ritual, which was composed for the Day of Atonement, contains a selection of his sublime and soul-stirring hymns.

C.Æ. 1154.—At Cordova, ABDELMUNEN BEN ALI ALKUMI ordered that all who refused to embrace Mohammedanism, whether Jews or Christians, were to quit the city. MAIMONIDES, who was then only nineteen years old, pretended to comply, but found means of escaping into Egypt.

" 1158.—The great MAIMONIDES, called Rabbi MOSES MAIMON, began his noted work, the *Yad H'chazokoh.* He also wrote in various Eastern languages and in Greek valuable treatises on medicine, astronomy, theology, philosophy, and logic. On his arrival at Egypt his great fame and learning caused him

CÆ. 1810.—MOSES MYERS became a member of the Legislature in South Carolina.

A motion to refuse admission to HENRY JACOBS, on religious grounds, after he had been returned as a member of the Legislature of North Carolina, was unanimously rejected.

" 1812.—FREDERICK III. repealed all oppressive laws against Jews in Prussia, and admitted them to civil liberty. They were also relieved from all disabilities by the Duke of Mecklenburg-Schwerin and the Prince Primate of Frankfort.

" 1813.—Civil rights granted to the Jews by the King of Bavaria. They were exempted from special imposts, and all trades and professions were open to them.

The United States of America appointed MORDECAI M. NOAH their consul at Tunis.

On the revolution in favor of the House of Orange, A. M. DE LEON and J. D. MEYER were made members of the commission at Amsterdam for securing order.

At Westphalia, Jews were only admitted who intended to establish manufactories, but those who were natives were allowed to possess land free of seignorial rights, and all schools were open to them.

MULEY SOLIMAN, Emperor of Morocco, appointed MASAHOD C. MACNIN envoy to the British government.

" 1814.—Denmark gave civil liberty and removed all restrictions against the Jews.

Jews compelled to quit the Free Cities of Lübeck and Bremen.

The city of Amsterdam elected A. MENDES DE LEON as Alderman.

The Order of the Belgic Lion conferred on J. D. MEYER, who was appointed secretary of the commission to form a new code for the kingdom of the Netherlands.

" 1815.—The Congress of Vienna adopted Article XVI., as follows: "The Congress will consider the best possible means of effecting a uniform amelioration of the followers of the Jewish religion throughout Germany, and particularly of granting them the enjoyment of civil rights in the Allied States, in return for their taking upon themselves all civil duties. Meanwhile, it guarantees to the professors of that faith the rights already granted them by the single States of the Alliance."

" 1817.—C. MEYER made referendary to the Ministry of Justice, and a Knight of the Belgic Lion.

1986.

Tishri	1	First Day of New Year	Saturday	Oct.	4
"	3	Fast of Gedaliah...............	Monday	"	6
"	10	Yom-Kippoor..................	Monday	"	13
"	15	First Day of Tabernacle.........	Saturday	"	18
"	21	Hoshannah-Rabbah.............	Friday	"	24
"	22	Sh'mini-Atseres...............	Saturday	"	25
"	23	Simchas-Torah.................	Sunday	"	26
Cheshvan.		Rosh-Chodesh	Sun.-Mon.	Nov.	2-3
Kislev	1	Rosh-Chodesh	Tues.-Wed.	Dec.	2-3
"	25	First Day of Chanukah..........	Saturday	"	27

1987.

Tebet	1	Rosh-Chodesh	Thurs.-Fri.	Jan.	1-2
"	10	Fast of Tebet..................	Sunday	"	11
Sh'vat	1	Rosh-Chodesh	Saturday	"	31
Adar.		Rosh-Chodesh	Sun -Mon.	Mar.	1-2
"	13	Fast of Esther.................	Saturday*	"	14
"	14-15	Purim...........	Sun.-Mon.	"	15-16
Nissan	1	Rosh-Chodesh	Tuesday	"	31
"	15	First Day of Passover	Tuesday	April	14
Iyar.		Rosh-Chodesh	Wed.-Thurs.	"	29-30
"	18	Lag-B'Omer	Sunday	May	17
		33d day of Omer.			
Sivan	1	Rosh-Chodesh	Friday	"	29
"	6	First Day of Pentecost............	Wednesday	June	3
Tammuz.		Rosh-Chodesh	Sat.-Sun.	"	27-28
"	17	Fast of Tammuz................	Tuesday	July	14
Av	1	Rosh-Chodesh	Monday	"	27
"	9	Fast of Av....................	Tuesday	Aug.	4
Ellul.		Rosh-Chodesh	Tues.-Wed.	"	25-26

* Observed Thursday previous.

EVENTFUL RECORDS.

to be appointed physician to the Sultan SALADIN. He died there at the age of seventy years, and is buried near Saphet. From his long residence in that country he was sometimes designated the Egyptian. So highly was he esteemed. and so great was his erudition, that the saying arose, "From MOSES unto MOSES there was none like MOSES."

C.Æ. 1160.—Pope ALEXANDER III. favored and defended the Jews. He desired that none should be allowed to disturb them on their Sabbaths or festivals, and appointed Rabbi YECHIEL as steward and overseer of his household and accounts. The Jews of Bagdad were much favored by MOSTANGED, who formed for them courts of justice under their own system and rabbis.

C.Æ. 1818.—An attempt was made to prevent Jews from attending the Leipsic Fair.

" 1819.—M. M. NOAH elected sheriff of the city of New York.

" 1820.—JOHN VI. admitted the Jews and granted them toleration at Lisbon.

  The Emperor of Morocco appointed JUDAH BENOLIEL, of Gibraltar, as consul, with power to appoint vice-consuls wherever he might consider it necessary.

" 1822.—NATHAN MEYER DE ROTHSCHILD made Baron of the Austrian Empire by Emperor FRANCIS I. and appointed Austrian consul, the title of baron being conferred upon his brothers. He was the founder of the British house of that noted family.

" 1824.—Knighthood of the Legion of Honor was conferred upon AARON CARDOZA, of Gibraltar, by LOUIS XVIII.

  J. BOAS was appointed one of the three magistrates of Amsterdam.

" 1825.—NATHAN LEVY made American consul to the island of St. Thomas.

  A fleet was sent against Morocco by Sardinia, but the differences were pacifically adjusted by JUDAH BENOLIEL, consul at Gibraltar.

" 1826.—It was reported by the CHEVALIER GAMBA that near Kouba, in Southern Russia, he found a Jewish village which had existed from an unknown time.

  The Jews of France were relieved from a ceremonial oath on the Books of the Law, which had formerly been exacted from them. This was accomplished by the eminent Jewish advocate, CRÉMIEUX, who defended Mons. GUERNON DE RANVILLE, ex-minister of CHARLES X.

  At Metz, a Jew was condemned simply because he had not taken the said oath, but Advocate OULIFF, also a Jew, obtained a reversal of the sentence.

" 1827.—Pope LEO XII. placed many restrictions upon the Jews at Rome.

  MORDECAI MYERS became a member of the Legislature of Georgia, U. S. A.

  MULEY ABD-ER-RAHMAN, Emperor of Morocco, appointed MEIR C. MACHNIN envoy to the British consul at St. James.

" 1828.—The Emperor NICHOLAS adopted various regulations concerning the Jews.

  Baron N. M. DE ROTHSCHILD was made Austrian Consul-General.

		1987.			
Tishri	1	First Day of New Year..........	Thursday	Sept.	24
"	3	Fast of Gedaliah................	Saturday*	"	26
"	10	Yom-Kippoor	Saturday	Oct.	3
"	15	First Day of Tabernacle	Thursday	"	8
"	21	Hoshannah-Rabbah	Wednesday	"	14
"	22	Sh'mini-Atseres.................	Thursday	"	15
"	23	Simchas-Torah	Friday	"	16
Cheshvan.		Rosh-Chodesh	Fri.-Sat.	"	23-24
Kislev	1	Rosh-Chodesh	Sunday	Nov.	22
"	25	First Day of Chanukah	Wednesday	Dec.	16
Tebet.		Rosh-Chodesh	Mon.-Tues.	"	21-22
"	10	Fast of Tebet	Thursday	"	31
		1988.			
Sh'vat	1	Rosh-Chodesh	Wednesday	Jan.	20
Adar.		Rosh-Chodesh	Thurs.-Fri.	Feb.	18-19
"	13	Fast of Esther.................	Wednesday	Mar.	2
"	14-15	Purim	Thurs.-Fri.	"	3-4
Nissan	1	Rosh-Chodesh	Saturday	"	19
"	15	First Day of Passover	Saturday	Apr.	2
Iyar.		Rosh-Chodesh	Sun.-Mon.	"	17-18
"	18	Lag-B'Omer...................	Thursday	May	5
		33d day of Omer.			
Sivan	1	Rosh-Chodesh	Tuesday	"	17
"	6	First Day of Pentecost	Sunday ·	"	22
Tammuz.		Rosh-Chodesh	Wed.-Thurs.	June 15-16	
"	17	Fast of Tammuz................	Saturday*	July	2
Av	1	Rosh-Chodesh	Friday	"	15
"	9	Fast of Av	Saturday*	"	23
Ellul.		Rosh-Chodesh	Sat.-Sun.	Aug. 13-14	

* Observed following day.

EVENTFUL RECORDS.

C.Æ. 1163.—On account of an accusation of killing a child for the Passover celebration, eighty-four Jews were burned at Paris.

The beautiful and sublime work, *Chovos Holvovos*, was written at Barcelona by Rabbi BECHAYAI the Elder.

" 1170.—The Jews were ordered by HENRY II. to leave England, but upon the payment of about $15,000 they were allowed to remain.

A Jew named JOSEPH was appointed Prime Minister by ALPHONSO VIII., who was deeply in love with a beautiful Jewess, which caused him to show great favor to the Jews. She fell a victim to the malice and ill-will of the court and clergy, who were jealous of her.

C.Æ. 1830.—In the British House of Commons, on April 5th, a bill passed its first reading, by a majority of 18, for the removal of all civil disabilities of the Jews.

May 17th. At the second reading it was lost by a majority of 63.

A resolution that the Jewish clergy be paid by the State was carried by a majority of 140 in the Chamber of Deputies in France, and confirmed by a majority of 52 in the Chamber of Peers.

At Norfolk, Va., U. S. A., MOSES MYERS was appointed collector of customs.

Knighthood of the Order of the Belgic Lion conferred upon J. MENDES DE LEON, alderman of Amsterdam.

"   1831.—Freedom of the city of London open to the Jews.

At Jamaica, ALEXANDER BRAVO and PHILIP LUCAS were appointed magistrates and assistant judges.

"   1832.—The like offices and distinctions given to JACOB DE PASS and ABRAHAM ISAACS.

SAMUEL JUDAH became a member of the Legislature of Indiana.

M. M. NOAH appointed Surveyor of the Port of New York.

The military order of WILLIAM of Holland given to M. BRANDON MONDOLPHO, first lieutenant of artillery.

CHAPMAN LEVY became a member of the Senate of South Carolina.

In England, ARTHUR LUMLEY DAVIDS, of extraordinary talents, died of cholera. At 15 years of age he had completed a Turkish grammar; he had acquired the Hebrew, Arabic, Persian, Turkish, French, Italian, and German languages. When only 18 years old he delivered some admirable lectures on the "Philosophy of the Jews," and was titled by some literary scholars the modern MENDELSOHN.

"   1833.—April 17th. A bill was again introduced into the British House of Commons for the removal of Jewish disabilities, and on its second reading, May 22d, was carried by a majority of 137.

June 26th. Its opponents at the third reading moved four amendments, which were lost by majorities of 93, 95, 84, and 91.

August 1st. A majority of 50 rejected it in the House of Lords.

"   1834.—It was again introduced and passed its various readings in the Commons.

		1988.			
Tishri	1	First Day of New Year	Monday	Sept.	12
"	3	Fast of Gedaliah................	Wednesday	"	14
"	10	Yom-Kippoor...................	Wednesday	"	21
"	15	First Day of Tabernacle.........	Monday	"	26
"	21	Hoshannah-Rabbah..............	Sunday	Oct.	2
"	22	Sh'mini-Atseres................	Monday	"	3
"	23	Simchas-Torah..................	Tuesday	"	4
Cheshvan.		Rosh-Chodesh	Tues.-Wed.	"	11-12
Kislev	1	Rosh-Chodesh	Thursday	Nov.	10
"	25	First Day of Chanukah..........	Sunday	Dec.	4
Tebet	1	Rosh-Chodesh..................	Friday	"	9
"	10	Fast of Tebet...................	Sunday	"	18
		1989.			
Sh'vat	1	Rosh-Chodesh	Saturday	Jan.	7
Adar.		Rosh-Chodesh	Sun.-Mon.	Feb.	5-6
2d Adar.		Rosh-Chodesh	Tues.-Wed.	Mar.	7-8
"	13	Fast of Esther.................	Monday	"	20
"	14-15	Purim......	Tues.-Wed.	"	21-22
Nissan	1	Rosh-Chodesh ....'.....	Thursday	Apr.	6
"	15	First Day of Passover...........	Thursday	"	20
Iyar.		Rosh-Chodesh	Fri.-Sat.	May	5-6
"	18	Lag-B'Omer .... 33d day of Omer.	Tuesday	"	23
Sivan	1	Rosh-Chodesh	Sunday	June	4
"	6	First Day of Pentecost..........	Friday	"	9
Tammuz.		Rosh-Chodesh	Mon.-Tues.	July	3-4
"	17	Fast of Tammuz	Thursday	"	20
Av	1	Rosh-Chodesh	Wednesday	Aug.	2
"	9	Fast of Av.....................	Thursday	"	10
Ellul.		Rosh-Chodesh	Thurs.-Fri.	{ " Sept.	31 1

EVENTFUL RECORDS.

CÆ. 1171.—Upon some unfounded pretext thirty-one Jews were burned at Calayatud.

At Granada, Rabbi MOSES BEN THIBON translated into Hebrew many of the works which MAIMONIDES had written in Arabic, including Euclid and Hippocrates. He also wrote several philosophical treatises of great value.

" 1178.—Permission was given to the Jews in England to have burial grounds outside of each city where they resided.

C.Æ. 1834.—June 23d.   Again lost in the House of Lords by a majority of 92.

B. FOULD made a member of the Chamber of Deputies for St. Quentin.

" 1835.—DAVID SALOMONS elected sheriff of London and Middlesex.

A French Jew bought landed property, which was refused registration by the city of Mülhausen because he was a Jew: for which LOUIS PHILIPPE, King of France, demanded and obtained satisfaction.

The King of Piedmont prohibited the Jews holding landed property, unless by his special license.

In London the citizens of Aldgate Ward elected Sheriff SALOMONS as alderman.

JACOB MONTEFIORE was elected a commissioner for South Australia.

The Order of the Legion of Honor couferred upon J. D. MYERS, of Amsterdam, by LOUIS PHILIPPE.

" 1836.—The King of the Netherlands conferred the knighthood of the Belgic Lion on J. DE CASTRO, alderman of The Hague.

J. TEIXERA NUNES made a member of the Equestrian Order of the Province of Holland.

May 31st.   The Chancellor of the Exchequer moved to go into committee "to consider the laws imposing civil disabilities on His Majesty's subjects professing the Jewish religion."

June 1st.   Resolution reported: "That it is expedient to remove all civil disabilities at present existing with respect to His Majesty's subjects professing the Jewish religion, with the like exceptions as are provided with respect to His Majesty's subjects professing the Roman Catholic religion."

June 13th.   Bill presented and read.

August 3d.   Bill read a second time.

August 15th.   Read the third time and passed in the House of Commons, and presented and read in the House of Lords.

August 19th.   The second reading postponed on the motion of the Marquess of Westminster.

B. FOULD re-elected a third time a member of the Chamber of Deputies for St. Quentin.

Emancipation of the Jews proposed to the States by the government of Hesse.

The cultivation of land prohibited to the Jews in Prussia, and all contracts with them ordered to be made in the presence of a magistrate.

Jews taking degrees in medicine in Russia declared eligible to be employed by the State.

		1989.			
Tishri	1	First Day of New Year	Saturday	Sept.	30
"	3	Fast of Gedaliah	Monday	Oct.	2
"	10	Yom-Kippoor	Monday	"	9
"	15	First Day of Tabernacle	Saturday	"	14
"	21	Hoshannah-Rabbah	Friday	"	20
"	22	Sh'mini-Atseres	Saturday	"	21
"	23	Simchas-Torah	Sunday	"	22
Cheshvan.		Rosh-Chodesh	Sun.-Mon.	"	29-30
Kislev.		Rosh-Chodesh	Tues.-Wed.	Nov.	28-29
"	25	First Day of Chanukah	Saturday	Dec.	23
Tebet.		Rosh-Chodesh	Thurs.-Fri.	"	28-29
		1990.			
"	10	Fast of Tebet	Sunday	Jan.	7
Sh'vat	1	Rosh-Chodesh	Saturday	"	27
Adar.		Rosh-Chodesh	Sun.-Mon.	Feb.	25-26
"	13	Fast of Esther	Saturday*	Mar.	10
"	14-15	Purim	Sun.-Mon.	"	11-12
Nissan	1	Rosh-Chodesh	Tuesday	"	27
"	15	First Day of Passover	Tuesday	Apr.	10
Iyar.		Rosh-Chodesh	Wed.-Thurs.	"	25-26
"	18	Lag-B'Omer. 33d day of Omer.	Sunday	May	13
Sivan	1	Rosh-Chodesh	Friday	"	25
"	6	First Day of Pentecost	Wednesday	"	30
Tammuz.		Rosh-Chodesh	Sat.-Sun.	June	23-24
"	17	Fast of Tammuz	Tuesday	July	10
Av	1	Rosh-Chodesh	Monday	"	23
"	9	Fast of Av	Tuesday	"	31
Ellul.		Rosh-Chodesh	Tues.-Wed.	Aug.	21-22

* Observed Thursday previous.

EVENTFUL RECORDS.

C.Æ. 1181.—Whilst in their synagogues on February 14th the Jews were seized and imprisoned by order of PHILIP AUGUSTUS, who cancelled all obligations due to them. Two months later, he confiscated all their immovable property, and decreed that they should leave France forthwith, which caused them to invent bills of exchange.*

" 1187.—SALADIN took Jerusalem.

" 1188.—To defray the expenses of the expedition of HENRY II. to the Holy Land, he ordered a levy of $300,000 upon the Jews, but it was not enforced, owing to his death.

* "Dictionnaire de Tremoux."

200

[Continued on page 131.]

C.Æ. 1836.—The Governor of Maryland appointed M. J. COHEN his aide-de-camp.

Lieutenant URIAH LEVY made a captain of the United States navy.

" 1837.—At Saphet and Tiberias, 5,000 Jews perished in an earthquake.

During the Viceroyalty of the Duke of Cambridge, the States of Hanover emancipated the Jews.

MOSES MONTEFIORE elected Sheriff of London and Middlesex, and knighted by Queen VICTORIA.

" 1838.—J. M. DE LEON and F. ASSER made members of the college for nominating the delegates of Amsterdam to the Provincial States of Holland.

ALEXANDER BRAVO made a member of the Queen's Council at Jamaica.

DAVID SALOMONS made a magistrate for the County of Kent, England.

In return for the munificent liberality of the Jews to the sufferers by inundation, the municipality of Ofen declared them free to become citizens and landholders.

The English Government ratified the hereditary title of Baron. to LIONEL, eldest son of N. M. DE ROTHSCHILD.

A Jew, for the first time, called to the bar of the Court of Chancery in England.

June 21st. Civil disabilities of the Jews removed.

" 1840.—The Jews were dreadfully persecuted at Damascus.

Sir MOSES MONTEFIORE went to Egypt in their behalf.

February 10th. SOLOMON J. HART was the first Jew elected a Royal Academician in England.

" 1841.—November 12th. The *Jewish Chronicle*, the first of the Anglo-Jewish press, established at London.

" 1842.—Opening of the first Reform Jewish Synagogue in London, with Rev., now Professor, DAVID W. MARKS as its Minister.

October 31st. Death of the Rev. SOLOMON HIRSCHELL, the venerated Chief Rabbi of Great Britain.

" 1845.—Installation of the Rev. Dr. NATHAN MARCUS ADLER as his successor.

" 1846.—Sir MOSES MONTEFIORE and Sir ANTHONY DE ROTHSCHILD made Baronets of the British Empire.

" 1847.—Baron LIONEL DE ROTHSCHILD elected member of Parliament for the City of London.

" 1851.—DAVID SALOMONS elected member of Parliament for Greenwich.

C.Æ. 1856.—DAVID SALOMONS was made Lord Mayor of London.

" 1857.—BENJAMIN S. PHILLIPS elected alderman for the City of London.

" 1858.—Jewish Oaths Bill passed in the House of Lords.
July 26th. Baron LIONEL DE ROTHSCHILD took his seat in Parliament.

" 1860.—Sir FRANCIS GOLDSMID elected a member of Parliament.

" 1865.—Alderman BENJAMIN S. PHILLIPS elected Lord Mayor of London, and knighted in the following year.
Mr. JOSEPH ABRAHAM, of Bristol, England, elected as its mayor.
In Australia, between 1858 and 1865, several Jews were elected to various important offices.
In Queensland, Mr. JULIUS VOGEL, who was afterwards knighted for eminent services, was Postmaster-General. In Sydney, New South Wales, there were several Jews in the Legislature, some of whom were in the Cabinet. In Melbourne they filled high civic positions, and Mr. EDWARD COHEN, for several years president of the Melbourne Hebrew Congregation, and an active member of all communal affairs, was elected mayor of the city and subsequently was Colonial Treasurer.
Amongst the members of the Colonial Parliament were Messrs. NATHANIEL LEVI, EPHRAIM ZOX, and others.

" 1866.—Professor ARTOM appointed Chief Rabbi of the Portuguese Jews in England.

" 1869.—NUMA HARTOG the first Jewish Senior Wrangler.
Mr. SEARJEANT SIMON elected M.P. for Dewsbury.
Mr. GEORGE JESSELL elected M.P. for Dover.
Mr. NATHANIEL M. DE ROTHSCHILD elected M.P. for Aylesbury.

" 1871.—The Messrs. WORMS created Barons.

" 1872.—Mr. GEORGE JESSELL appointed Solicitor-General for England, and knighted.
Mr. ALBERT SASSOON knighted.
The University Test Bill passed in England.
Congress at Washington opened with prayer by the Rev. ABRAHAM DE SOLA, of Montreal.

" 1873.—The freedom of the City of London presented to Sir A. SASSOON, C.S.I.
Sir GEORGE JESSELL appointed Master of the Rolls. He closed his Court on *Yom-Kippur*, the day of Atonement.

C.Æ. 1879.—Death of Professor ARTOM and Baron LIONEL DE ROTHSCHILD.

" 1881.—H.R.H. the PRINCE OF WALES visited the Central Synagogue in London, to attend the marriage of Mr. LEOPOLD DE ROTH-SCHILD to Miss PERUIGIA, on January 19th.

" 1882.—Violent outbreaks occurred against the Jews in various parts of Russia, and many thousands were obliged to flee. Gross and inhuman outrages were committed on the unoffending victims, neither age nor sex being spared. They were kindly received in England and many European cities and foreign countries. Several thousands emigrated to the United States of America, where the utmost sympathy and most substantial aid were afforded them. Christian as well as Jewish communities in distant lands evinced their sympathies by practical and substantial assistance.

" 1883.—Death of Sir GEORGE JESSELL, Master of the Rolls in England, March 21st.

Mr. H. A. ISAACS, Common Councilman, elected Alderman of London.

" 1884.—Death of the Baroness LIONEL DE ROTHSCHILD, who was renowned for her unbounded and unsectarian charities, and for her personal and active interest in the management of the Jewish Infant and Free Schools, to which she was a frequent visitor.

EDWARD LASKER, a Liberal leader in the German Parliament, died whilst on a visit to his brother in the United States. His remains were sent to Germany for interment, and all classes joined in paying honor to the deceased Jewish statesman. The American House of Representatives gracefully sent resolutions of condolence to the German Reichstag, but Prince BISMARCK, LASKER's political enemy, refused to accept and present them, on the grounds that by so doing he would stultify his principles, which were opposed to LASKER's; and that Herr LASKER's position in the Reichstag was not sufficiently important to call for them.

" 1885.—The venerable and world-renowned philanthropist and champion of liberty, Sir MOSES MONTEFIORE, died shortly after the celebration of his 100th birthday.

Lieutenant-Colonel PHILIP COWAN elected alderman of London.

Mr. FAUDEL PHILLIPS elected Sheriff of London and Middlesex.

Sir NATHANIEL DE ROTHSCHILD, M.P., eldest son of Baron LIONEL, elevated to the peerage of England, with the title of LORD DE ROTHSCHILD.

C.Æ.   1885.—Baron HENRY DE WORMS, M.P., appointed Parliamentary Secretary to the British Board of Trade, England.

"   1887.—Alderman and Sheriff ISAACS knighted.

Rev. Dr. GASTER appointed Chief Rabbi of the Portuguese in England.

Special services to celebrate the Jubilee of Queen VICTORIA held in all the London synagogues.

Death of Mr. LIONEL COHEN, M.P., an active and indefatigable worker and promoter of all Jewish interests.

Death of Sir BARROW ELLIS, K.C.S.I.

"   1889.—Lord ROTHSCHILD appointed Lord Lieutenant and Custos Rotulorum for the County of Buckingham.

"   1890.—The Rev. Dr. NATHAN MARCUS ADLER, Chief Rabbi of the United Kingdom and British Dominions, died at Brighton after an administration of forty-five years.

The Russian Government ordered the enforcement of the edicts of 1882 against the Jews. These edicts had hitherto been held in abeyance. According to them Jews may henceforth only reside in certain towns. None are permitted to own land or hire it for agricultural purposes. The order includes several towns and hundreds of villages which have large Jewish populations. No Jew is to be allowed to hold shares in or work in mines. The law limiting the residence of Jews to sixteen provinces will be enforced. No Jew will be allowed to enter the army, to practise medicine or law, to be an engineer, or to enter any other professions, and they will be debarred from holding posts under the government.

BARON DE HIRSCH, of Paris, through whose unbounded benevolence many educational and industrial schools were established in Egypt and European and Asiatic Turkey, gave 10,000,000 francs ($2,000,000) for educational purposes in Gallicia. Subsequently, he made to the Russian government the munificent offer of $10,000,000 for public instruction, with the sole stipulation that the fund should be applied

"   1891. without distinction of creed or race, which unparalleled act of generosity was refused by bigoted Russia. Baron de Hirsch gave $240,000 for the amelioration of the condition of Jewish refugees in the United States, placing the fund in the hands of a committee of prominent and influential gentlemen in New York, who were well known for their active and disinterested works of benevolence and their capacity to carry out so responsible a task. The Baron's intention is not to pauperize the recipients of his charity, but, after having sup-

C.Æ. 1891   plied their immediate necessities and established schools. to place them on small farms and teach them trades so as to make them self-dependent. To Canada, the Baron sent $20,000 to the Young Men's Hebrew Benevolent Society at Montreal for the assistance of refugees arriving there from barbarous Russia, and there are many other instances of his great liberality. The private charities of the Baron and his estimable wife are on a par with their public benefactions, and they not only give lavishly to those who need, but personally investigate the circumstances of applicants, with the view of giving them *practical* aid. Wherever help is required the Baron and his wife make no distinction as to religion or race.

The Rev. Dr Herman Adler, of London, England, elected Chief Rabbi of Great Britain and the British Dominions.

www.ingramcontent.com/pod-product-compliance
Lightning Source LLC
Chambersburg PA
CBHW020619030726
47497CB00007B/2323